mental health
(care and treatment) (scotland) act 2003

code of practice

volume 2 –
civil compulsory powers
(parts 5, 6, 7 & 20)

ISBN 0 7559 4568 9

Published by
Scottish Executive
St Andrew's House
Edinburgh
EH1 3DG

Produced for the Scottish Executive by Astron B37403 07-05

Published by the Scottish Executive, July, 2005

Further copies are available from
Blackwell's Bookshop
53 South Bridge
Edinburgh
EH1 1YS

This document is printed on chlorine-free, acid-free, recyclable and bio-degradable paper.

table of contents

Chapter 4: The compulsory treatment order and the interim compulsory treatment order in operation (Part 7, Chapters 2, 3 & 7)

Chapter 5: Reviewing a compulsory treatment order (Part 7, Chapter 4)

Chapter 6: Non-compliance with a community-based compulsory treatment order or interim compulsory treatment order (Part 7, Chapter 5)

introduction

to volume 2

introduction

Coverage of this volume

01 Volume 2 of the Code of Practice for the Mental Health (Care and Treatment) (Scotland) Act 2003 ("the Act") deals with a range of issues relating to what can be termed "civil compulsory powers". It therefore provides Code of Practice material on Parts 5, 6, 7 and 20 of the Act which relate to an emergency detention certificate; a short-term detention certificate; an extension certificate; a compulsory treatment order; an interim compulsory treatment order; and absconding from any of these certificates/orders.

02 This volume does not look at the procedures surrounding the compulsory care and treatment of a person with a mental disorder who has committed any form of criminal offence. These procedures are set out in Parts 8 to 13 of the Act and are examined in volume 3 of the Code of Practice.

03 This volume, similarly, does not examine a range of other subjects for which provision is made in the Act. These subjects include, for example, detention in conditions of excessive security (Part 17 Chapter 3); cross-border transfers of patients (section 289 and 290); the duties of Health Boards and local authorities (Part 4); the provision of advocacy services (section 259). These issues are discussed in volume 1 of the Code of Practice.

Structure of this volume

04 This volume is divided into 11 chapters.

05 Chapter 1 provides an overview to this volume by describing the principles of the Act before providing definitions of 2 keys terms: that is, "mental disorder" and "medical treatment". It then provides an overview of the civil compulsory powers available as well as a discussion of the criteria which must be met before these powers can be exercised.

introduction

06 Chapter 2 examines the procedures which must be followed when granting a short-term detention certificate under Part 6 of the Act. The chapter adopts a chronological approach to the relevant procedures moving from the point at which the person presents with a suspected mental disorder to the point at which the detention certificate is granted and the person is admitted to hospital. It also examines processes relating to the revocation and the suspension of a short-term detention certificate.

07 Chapters 3 to 6 focus on the "compulsory treatment order" (CTO). This is an order which can be made under Part 7 of the Act and which authorises compulsory treatment for a period of at least 6 months at a time. These four chapters also adopt a chronological approach as they start from the point at which it appears to the relevant parties that an application for a CTO might be appropriate before progressing to the point at which a CTO is reviewed and/or revoked.

08 Chapter 3, therefore, describes the processes by which an application for a CTO is made. It covers, for example, the medical practitioners' preparation of mental health reports as a prelude to the preparation of the application, including the proposed care plan and mental health officer's report, by an MHO. The chapter also describes the process by which this application is determined by the Mental Health Tribunal for Scotland ("the Tribunal").

09 Chapter 4 deals with issues relating to a CTO and an interim CTO once it is in operation and the procedures which should follow on immediately from it being made, including the preparation of a care plan and the processes by which the compulsory measures specified in a CTO or an interim CTO can be suspended.

10 Chapter 5 describes the processes associated with reviewing and revoking a CTO, including the making of "a section 86 determination" to extend a CTO; "a section 92 application" to extend a CTO with a variation of its terms; and "a section 95 application" to vary the terms of the CTO. The chapter also examines applications to the Tribunal by the patient and the patient's named person.

introduction

11 Chapter 6 examines the procedures to be followed where a patient has not complied with any of the compulsory measures which are specified in a community-based CTO or interim CTO.

12 Chapter 7 examines the procedures to be followed when granting an emergency detention certificate under Part 5 of the Act. The chapter adopts a chronological approach to the relevant procedures moving from the point at which the person presents with a suspected mental disorder to the point at which the detention certificate is granted and the person admitted to hospital. It also examines the processes relating to the revocation and the suspension of an emergency detention certificate.

13 Chapter 8 focuses on the provisions of the Act which relate to patients who abscond while subject to the civil compulsory powers outlined in this volume.

14 Chapter 9 turns to the procedures to be followed where a patient who is subject to civil compulsory powers is being transferred from one hospital to another within Scotland. *(For further information on the procedures to be followed where a patient is being transferred in or out of Scotland, see Chapter 14 of Volume 1 of the Code of Practice.)*

15 Chapter 10 provides a glossary of important terms and abbreviations which are commonly used throughout this volume and the other 2 volumes of the Code of Practice.

16 Chapter 11 gives a list of non-statutory forms. Although there is no statutory requirement to use these forms, you are strongly recommended to do so. The forms draw attention to some procedural requirements under the Act. Failure to observe procedural requirements may invalidate either the application or certificate or report, etc. Non-statutory forms can be found on the Commission's website at www.mwcscot.org.uk Statutory forms are to be found on the Mental Health Law website at www.scotland.gov.uk/health/mentalhealthlaw

introduction

Abbreviations and other commonly used terms

17 Although the use of abbreviations has been avoided wherever possible in the Code Practice, the following are used commonly throughout this volume:

• **Commission**	• Mental Welfare Commission
• **CPN**	• Community psychiatric nurse
• **CTO**	• Compulsory treatment order
• **DMP**	• Designated medical practitioner
• **ICTO**	• Interim compulsory treatment order
• **MHO**	• Mental health officer
• **RMO**	• Responsible medical officer
• **Tribunal**	• The Mental Health Tribunal for Scotland

18 The following pieces of legislation are also on occasion referred to in an abbreviated form:

• **"the 1995 Act"**	• Criminal Procedure (Scotland) Act 1995
• **"the 2000 Act"**	• Adults with Incapacity (Scotland) Act 2000
• **"the Act"**	• Mental Health (Care and Treatment) (Scotland) Act 2003

The Act should be read in conjunction with all subordinate legislation made under the Act. The Code of Practice refers to the regulations, orders and directions made under the Act at appropriate points.

Readers should be aware in particular of two orders made under the Act – The Mental Health (Care and Treatment) (Scotland) Act 2003 Modification Order 2004 (SSI No. 533) and The Mental Health (Care and Treatment) (Scotland) Act 2003 (Modification of Enactments) Order 2005 – which have amended the Act.

The Code points out where important changes have been made but practitioners may be advised to check the relevant orders themselves and to seek their own legal advice as required, when referring to the relevant provisions of the Act.

At the time of drafting this version of the Code, some of the regulations and orders referred to have not yet been approved by the Scottish Parliament. It was felt that nonetheless it was helpful to the reader to include references prospectively. Practitioners are advised to check the mental health pages on the Scottish Executive website for current information and links to the latest versions of subordinate legislation on OPSI.

19 Certain terms which are used regularly throughout this volume have a specific meaning in the context of the Act which it is important to note. Although these terms are defined in section 329 of the Act, it is worthwhile repeating some of them here.

• **"notice"/"notify"**	• notice in writing
• **"patient"**	• a person who has or who appears to have a mental disorder
• **"regulations"**	• secondary legislation which is made by the Scottish Ministers under the Act in terms of section 326

Good practice versus best practice

20 The phrase "best practice" has been used throughout this Code of Practice in preference to the phrase "good practice". This is to provide consistency with the duty placed on the Commission by way of section 5 of the Act to "promote best practice" in relation to the operation of the Act. The use of the term "best practice" does not imply that any of the activities or duties described in that way are purely aspirational or less likely to be achieved than an activity or duty which might elsewhere be described as being indicative of "good practice".

introduction

Patient confidentiality

21 The section 1 principles also require that any decision or course of action being considered (other than a decision about medical treatment) should as far as practical and reasonable take into account the needs and circumstances of the patient's carer and the importance of providing such information to any carer as might assist the carer to care for the patient. However, when a person is considering the information to be shared with the carer, it would be best practice to consider in every case the patient's right to confidentiality about their private medical details and treatment options, before information is supplied. It should also be noted that the Community Care and Health (Scotland) Act 2002 amends the Social Work (Scotland) Act 1968 to give carers a right to have their carer needs assessed by the local authority. It would be best practice to bring this assessment right to the notice of any carer providing a substantial amount of care where the carer appears to have unmet caring needs.

Interpretation of timescales

22 The Act uses a number of ways of counting the time period in relation to Orders, etc. In all cases, the relevant section of the Act is specific about how these time periods should be counted.

23 Where the Act specifies a number of hours, these should be counted in hours from the time of signing the certificate etc. Examples of this are the period of 72 hours provided for at section 36(8) and in section 44(5)(a) where the Act says the 'period beginning with the granting of the certificate'.

24 Where the Act specifies a number of days or weeks beginning at a certain point these are counted from the beginning of the first day of the period. Examples of this are the period of 3 days provided for at section 44(5)(a) and the 7 day period in section 45(3)(b) where the Act states 'before the expiry of the 7 day period beginning with the day on which the MHO is consulted…', and the period of 28 days provided for at section 44(5)(b where the Act says 'a period of 28 days beginning with …the beginning of the day on which …'.

25 The Act also provides at some points for time periods (generally months or years) ending at a specific time. For example, section 165 states 'the period of two years ending with the day on which the order would have ceased to authorise these measures…'. This period will be counted back from the beginning of the day on which the order ceases to have effect.

26 At some sections the Act specifically says 'working' days. Section 47(8) of the Act defines a 'working day' as a day which is not:
  (a) Saturday
  (b) Sunday
  (c) a day which is a bank holiday under the Banking and Financial Dealings Act 1971 in Scotland.

27 At all other places where the Act mentions days, weeks or months these are calendar days, weeks, months as appropriate.

chapter one
overview

chapter one

Introduction

This chapter begins with the definition of mental disorder and medical treatment and then other matters which underpin the legislation and which are laid out at sections 1 to 3 of the Act. The two important terms used commonly throughout the Act: namely, “mental disorder” and “medical treatment”.

The chapter then gives a brief overview of the three principal certificates and orders in this Act on the authority of which a person may be detained: namely, an emergency detention certificate, a short-term detention certificate; and a compulsory treatment order.

This chapter also examines some issues relating to the criteria which must be met before compulsory powers can be used. For example, it looks at what is meant by ‘significant impairment of decision-making ability’ and contrasts this with the term ‘incapacity’.

Finally, this chapter provides some clarification regarding the detention of children under this Act as well as regarding the expiry point of detention certificates and orders.

Definition of “mental disorder”

01 The Act refers throughout to a “patient”. In terms of section 329 of the Act, “patient” means a person who has or appears to have a mental disorder.

02 Section 328 of the Act provides that “mental disorder” means any mental illness, personality disorder, or learning disability, however caused or manifested.

03 The definition of mental disorder has been drawn widely to ensure that the services provided for in the Act are available to anyone who needs them. A person with mental disorder will only be subject to compulsory measures under the Act if they meet the specific criteria for those measures. However, section 25 to 27 of the Act also provides for a range of local authority duties in relation to the provision of services for any person who has or has had a mental disorder.

chapter one

04 Section 328(2) of the Act specifically states that a person is not mentally disordered by reason only of any of the following:

- sexual orientation;
- sexual deviancy;
- trans-sexualism;
- transvestism;
- dependence on, or use of, alcohol or drugs;
- behaviour that causes, or is likely to cause, harassment, alarm or distress to any other person;
- or by acting as no prudent person would act.

05 No person who suffers from mental disorder but also falls within any of the above categories should be excluded from consideration for assistance, treatment or services under the Act. For example, the provisions of the Act may be invoked in respect of people with mental disorder who also have alcohol problems or misuse drugs. Section 328(2) ensures that a person is not regarded as mentally disordered *by reason only* of their sexual orientation, deviancy, trans-sexualism, transvestism, dependence on drugs or alcohol, or by their behaviour.

chapter one

Definition of "medical treatment"

06 Section 329 of the Act defines "medical treatment" as "treatment for mental disorder; and for this purpose "treatment" includes-

- nursing;
- care;
- psychological intervention;
- habilitation (including education, and training in work, social and independent living skills); and
- rehabilitation (read in accordance with the paragraph above)".

07 "Medical treatment" includes pharmacological interventions as well as other physical interventions (such as electro-convulsive therapy (ECT)) in addition to psychological and social interventions (including occupational therapy) made with respect to mental disorder. Any references to "medical treatment" in the Act and this Code of Practice should be read in light of the definition in section 329 as outlined above.

08 Medical treatment for an unrelated physical disorder is not authorised by the Act. However, medical treatment for a physical disorder which is directly causing the mental disorder would be authorised. For example, where a patient has delirium (as a mental disorder secondary to a chest infection), then the administration of antibiotics would be a medical treatment (indirectly) for the mental disorder and so authorised by the Act. Other medically induced mental disorders could include starvation-induced depression, or hypothyroidism-induced depression. Self-harm (including overdose) as a result of a mental disorder may also be treated under the Act.

09 Where medical treatment for an unrelated medical disorder is required, and the patient is an adult and incapable of giving consent, then treatment under the Adults with Incapacity (Scotland) Act 2000 should be considered.

10 For further information on treating patients subject to an Emergency Detention certificate, see Chapter 7 of this Volume of the Code of Practice. For further information on "medical treatment", see also Part 16 of the Act and Chapter 10 of Volume 1 of the Code of Practice.

chapter one

Overview of the civil compulsory powers

11 There are three principal "civil" certificates and orders under this Act. These are:
- an emergency detention certificate which grants an authority to detain a person in hospital for a period of 72 hours;
- a short-term detention certificate which grants an authority to detain a person in hospital for a period of 28 days; and
- a compulsory treatment order (CTO) which grants an authority to exercise a range of compulsory powers over a person either in hospital or in the community for a period of 6 months. This period can be extended by 6 months, then by periods of 12 months thereafter.

12 A CTO can only be made by the Tribunal. A short-term detention certificate can only be issued by an approved medical practitioner while an emergency detention certificate can be issued by any registered medical practitioner.

13 Mental health officers (MHO) play a key role in the use of compulsory powers. For example, an MHO prepares an application for a CTO and the consent of an MHO must be obtained before a short-term detention certificate can be granted. The consent of an MHO must also be sought where it is practicable to do so before an emergency detention certificate can be granted.

14 The Act also provides for a range of other compulsory measures. These include a power of entry to the premises of a mentally disordered person and the removal of a mentally disordered person to a place of safety. These powers are not, however, described in this volume but are described in Volume 1 of the Code of Practice. Volume 3 similarly sets out procedures to be followed with respect to mentally disordered offenders.

Interaction between emergency and short-term detention certificates

15 It should be noted that a person can be made subject to a short-term detention certificate without the need to have been subject to an emergency detention certificate beforehand.

16 A short-term detention certificate should be granted, wherever possible, in preference to an emergency detention certificate, where this is practicable and where the relevant detention criteria have been met. A short-term detention certificate is the preferred "gateway order" because, as compared with an emergency detention certificate, it can only be granted by an approved medical practitioner; the consent of an MHO to the granting of a short-term detention certificate is mandatory; and it confers on the patient and the patient's named person a more extensive set of rights, including the right to make an application to the Tribunal to revoke the certificate.

17 When any decision about whether or not to grant an emergency or short-term detention certificate is being made, the difference in the criteria for emergency and short-term detention, as set out in sections 36 and 44 of the Act respectively, is paramount. In addition to these criteria, practitioners may also wish to consider other factors before deciding on whether it would be more appropriate to grant an emergency detention certificate or a short-term detention certificate. These could include:

- whether urgent action must be taken, and whether there is, as a result of this urgency, insufficient time to comply with the more extensive procedures allied to the granting of a short-term detention certificate;
- whether the medical practitioner is satisfied that the assessment for treatment could not be made with the patient's consent;
- whether an approved medical practitioner or an MHO is immediately or directly available to grant or consent to the granting of a short-term detention certificate.

18 Where the clinical urgency of the situation will not permit the granting of a short-term detention certificate, it should be borne in mind that the primary purpose of an emergency detention certificate is to permit a full assessment of a person's mental state. It is not to administer medical treatment for the suspected mental disorder. Such treatment may, however, be given where it is urgently required under the authority of section 243 of the Act.

chapter one

Criteria for civil compulsory power

19 Compulsory powers can only be exercised under the Act where strict criteria have been met. For details of the criteria which must be met before the various certificates and orders may be granted, see the relevant Part of the Act. Taking the example of a short-term detention certificate, such a certificate may only be granted where the approved medical practitioner considers it likely that the following criteria have been met:

- the patient has a mental disorder;
- the patient's ability to make decisions about the provision of medical treatment is significantly impaired as a result of that mental disorder;
- it is necessary to detain the patient in hospital for the purpose of determining what medical treatment should be given to the patient or of giving them medical treatment;
- there would be a significant risk to the health, safety or welfare of the patient or to the safety of any other person if the patient were not detained in hospital; and
- the granting of a short-term detention certificate is necessary.

20 It should be noted that all the criteria listed in the previous paragraph must be met before a short-term detention certificate can be granted. It should also be noted that the onus does not rest on the patient to prove that he/she does not in fact meet these criteria; the onus rests instead on the practitioner to demonstrate that he/she considers it likely that the above criteria are indeed met.

21 Two criteria in the list at paragraph 19 deserve particular mention. The final criterion is that the granting of a short-term detention certificate is necessary. This means that the patient must be unwilling to agree to admission to hospital and medical treatment on an informal or voluntary basis.

22 The second criterion in the list of criteria at paragraph 19 above concerns the concept of significantly impaired decision-making ability. This concept is separate to that of "incapacity" as defined under the Adults with Incapacity (Scotland) Act 2000. However, when assessing a person's decision-making ability, it is likely that similar factors will be considered to those taken into account when assessing incapacity. Such factors could involve consideration of the extent to which the person's mental disorder might adversely affect their ability to believe, understand and retain information concerning their care and treatment, to make decisions based on that information, and to communicate those decisions to others.

23 One difference between incapacity and significantly impaired decision-making ability arguably is that the latter is primarily a disorder of the mind in which a decision is made, resulting in the decision being made on the basis of reasoning coloured by a mental disorder. Incapacity, by contrast, broadly involves a disorder of brain and cognition which implies actual impairments or deficits which prevent or disrupt the decision-making process.

24 Moreover, significantly impaired decision-making ability must always be linked to the patient's mental disorder. Incapacity, by contrast, is defined at section 1 of the Adults with Incapacity (Scotland) Act 2000 and includes incapacity by reason of physical disability.

25 It is important to emphasise that the criterion listed at paragraph 19 above with respect to a significant impairment of decision-making ability means a significant impairment with respect to decisions about the provision of medical treatment for mental disorder.

26 Significantly impaired decision-making ability must always be as a result of mental disorder, but it should not necessarily be taken to be synonymous with mental disorder.

27 A person's decision-making ability should not be considered to be significantly impaired by reason only of a lack or deficiency in a faculty of communication. Similarly, it should not be taken as equivalent to disagreeing with the opinions of professionals.

chapter one

Can a child be made subject to civil compulsory powers?

28 Yes, a child under the age of 18 years can be made subject to an emergency or short-term detention certificate or a compulsory treatment order in the same way as an adult, and the procedures for granting or making such a certificate or order are the same irrespective of whether the patient is a child or an adult. Where it becomes apparent that it may be appropriate to grant, for example, an emergency detention certificate with respect to a child, special consideration should be given to the effects of detention on the child and to ensuring that all other options have been fully explored. While these points are, of course, also relevant to the detention of adults, they should be given particular consideration where a child is being detained.

29 For these purposes, a child is someone under the age of 18. It should further be noted section 2 requires that where a function is being discharged with respect to a child, it should be discharged in a manner "that best secures the welfare of the patient". Best practice would be for the RMO responsible for the child's care to be a child specialist.

30 If there is no option but detention, it would be best practice to admit the child, wherever possible, to a unit specialising in child and adolescent psychiatry. Practitioners are reminded of the requirement which section 23(1)(b) of the Act places on Health Boards to provide "such services and accommodation as are sufficient for the particular needs of that child or young person".

31 If the detained child cannot be admitted to a unit specialising in child and adolescent psychiatry, special consideration should always be given to the environment to which they are to be admitted. Any risks to the child should be identified in advance and a plan put in place to minimise such risks. This could entail, for example, prioritising the allocation of a single room and making special arrangements to monitor the child's general well-being within the ward environment. Particular consideration should also be given to the likely impact on the child or young person of the behaviour of other patients on the ward. Status should be given to the need to protect them from exposure to distressing experiences or potential risk. While these points are, of course, also very relevant to the detention of adults, they should be given particular consideration where a child is being detained.

32 Where a child/adolescent subject to compulsory powers is in an adult ward, it would be expected that the relevant hospital managers would notify the Mental Welfare Commission of this fact to enable it to monitor the provision of age-appropriate services under the Act.

33 Persons discharging functions under the Act are also reminded of the provisions of section 278 of the Act. That section applies where a child or a person with parental responsibilities is subject to any provisions of this Act or the 1995 Children (Scotland) Act. It states that persons discharging functions under these Acts must take all practicable and appropriate steps to mitigate any effects of the measures authorised by the Acts which might impair the personal relations or diminish direct contact between a child and a person with parental responsibilities. The patient's designated MHO will play a particularly important role in this process, particularly in relation to liaising closely with colleagues in social work children and families' teams.

chapter one

Interpretation of expiry of compulsory power

34 The various detention certificates and orders which can be granted or made under the Act have time limits. Taking the example of a short-term detention certificate, two powers are authorised. The first is the power to remove the patient to hospital or to a different hospital. Section 44(5)(a) of the Act states that this removal must take place "before the expiry of the period of 3 days beginning with the granting of the short-term detention certificate". The time limit runs from the exact time at which the event occurs: in this case the granting of the certificate. Therefore, if a short-term detention certificate is granted at 6pm on Monday, the removal to hospital must have taken place by 6pm on Thursday.

35 The second power authorised by a short-term detention certificate is a power under section 44(5)(b) of the Act to detain the patient in hospital for a period of 28 days. If the patient is already in hospital, the time limit will run from the beginning of the day on which the certificate is granted (see section 44(5)(b)(ii)). If the patient is being transferred from the community the time limit will run from the beginning of the day on which the patient is admitted to hospital (see section 44(5)(b)(i)). Therefore, for the purposes of section 44(5)(b), the time period runs from the beginning of the first day rather than the exact time at which the event took place. The whole day on which the event occurs is included in the calculation. For example, if a patient is admitted to hospital under a short-term detention certificate at 6pm on 2 January, the power to detain the patient in hospital begins at 00.00 midnight of 2 January (that is, during the night of 1 and 2 January) and expires at 00.00 (midnight) of 30 January (that is, during the night of 29 and 30 January). All other references in the Act to the expiry point of compulsory powers should be read in this light.

chapter 2
short-term detention certificate (part 6)

chapter two

Introduction

This chapter sets out the procedures which must be followed where the granting of a short-term detention certificate is being considered in accordance with the provisions of Part 6 of the Act. As stated in Chapter 1, short-term detention is the preferred "gateway order" to compulsory powers.

The chapter begins with a general overview of the provisions which relate to the granting of a certificate as a means of establishing the framework in which short-term detention operates.

The remainder of the chapter traces the specific procedures which must be gone through for a valid short-term detention certificate to be granted, extended and suspended.

At the end of the chapter, a flowchart illustrates the process by which a medical practitioner grants a short-term detention certificate.

Overview of short-term detention

How long does a period of short-term detention last?

01 The detention period is 28 days.

02 If a patient is not in hospital before the certificate is granted, the granting of the certificate authorises two separate procedures. These are:

- the patient's transfer to hospital. This transfer must take place within 3 days of the certificate being granted; and
- the patient's detention in hospital for a further 28 days.

03 *For further information with respect to how these time periods should be interpreted, see paragraph 20 of Chapter 1 of this Volume of the Code of Practice.*

04 The granting of a short-term detention certificate does not in itself authorise the patient's detention in hospital where the patient was in the community before the certificate was granted. The detention is only authorised when the short-term detention certificate has been given to the managers of the hospital in which the patient is to be detained before the patient is admitted to the hospital. Therefore, with respect to a patient who was in the community prior to the certificate being granted, the 28 day detention period begins with the patient's admission to hospital under the authority of the certificate.

chapter two

05 If the patient is already in hospital before the certificate is granted, he/she may only be detained for a period of 28 days from the beginning of the day on which the certificate is granted.

06 Although a short-term detention certificate authorises a 28 day period of hospital detention, it should not be assumed that the patient is always to be detained for the full 28 days. The detention certificate must be revoked if the relevant detention criteria are no longer met.

07 A short-term detention certificate can only be extended in two ways:
- by an extension certificate granted under section 47 of the Act; or
- by the 5 working days extension period permitted by section 68 of the Act where an application has been made for a compulsory treatment order.

08 *For further information on these extensions, see paragraphs 79 to 91 of this chapter.*

When can a short-term detention certificate be granted?

09 A short-term detention certificate can be granted where the criteria set out at section 44 of the Act have been met. It is important to note that a short-term detention certificate can be granted in respect of a patient who was immediately beforehand not subject to an emergency detention certificate.

10 A short-term detention certificate should be granted in preference to an emergency detention certificate, where this is practicable and where the relevant detention criteria have been met. *For further information on this point, see the section on the "overview of the civil compulsory powers" in Chapter 1 of this Volume of the Code of Practice.*

Who cannot be made subject to a short-term detention certificate?

11 Section 44(1) and (2) of the Act state that a short-term detention certificate may not be granted in respect of a patient who was subject to any of the following authorities to detain immediately before being examined for the purpose of the granting of the short-term detention certificate:
- a short-term detention certificate;
- an extension certificate granted under section 47 of the Act;
- section 68 of the Act;
- a certificate issued under sections 114(2) or 115(2) of the Act.

chapter two

Who has the authority to grant a short-term detention certificate?

12 A short-term detention certificate may only be granted by an approved medical practitioner (that is, a practitioner approved by a Health Board under section 22 of this Act).

Conflicts of interest with respect to short-term detention

13 Section 44(1) and (3) state that a short-term detention certificate may only be granted where there is no conflict of interest with respect to the medical examination. Section 44(8) provides a regulation-making power to define what is meant in this context by a conflict of interest. (See **The Mental Health (Conflict of Interest) (Scotland) (No 2) Regulations 2005 (SSI No. 262)**).

Those regulations state that a conflict of interest may exist where the approved medical practitioner is:

short-term detention –

- related to the patient in any degree (see prohibited degree of relationship below)
- employed by, or contracted to provide services in or to, an independent health care service in which the patient will be detained

compulsory treatment –

- either practitioner is related to the patient (see prohibited degrees of relationship below)
- the two medical practitioners are related to each other in any degree (see prohibited degrees of relationship below)
- where it is proposed the CTO treatment authorise detention of the patient in an independent health care service and either medical practitioner is employed by or contracted to provide services in or to that hospital

Prohibited degrees of relationship are:

- child, grandchild, parent, grandparent, wife, husband, sister, brother, daughter-in-law, son-in-law, mother-in-law, father-in-law, sister-in-law, brother-in law, cohabitee or family of the cobabitee

chapter two

14 There are, however, circumstances where there will not be considered a conflict of interest for a short-term detention. These are where the failure to carry out the medical examination by the approved medical examiner would result in a delay which would involve serious risk to the health, safety and welfare of the patient or to the safety of other persons.

15 In addition, if one of the medical practitioners is a consultant, the other medical practitioner must not work directly with or under the supervision of that consultant.

16 It would be best practice in such circumstances for the RMO to record the conflict(s) of interest which exist and their reason for their involvement in the short-term detention.

17 Although the Act makes no reference to conflicts of interest which may arise in relation to the MHOs involvement in the detention process, an MHO should nonetheless bear in mind that it would be best practice to avoid becoming involved in the detention of a colleague, close relative or friend, etc. An MHO who believes that a conflict of interest might arise in relation to the proposed detention should request his/her local authority employers to allocate another MHO to deal with the case.

Does the patient have a right of appeal against short-term detention?

18 Yes. The patient and the patient's named person both have a right to apply to the Tribunal under section 50 for a revocation of the short-term detention certificate. *Further information on this provision can be found in paragraphs 72 to 75 of this chapter.*

19 The Mental Welfare Commission also has a power to revoke a short-term detention certificate under section 51 of the Act. *Further information on this provision can be found in paragraphs 76 to 78 of this chapter.*

chapter two

Are the detention procedures relating to hospital in-patients different from those relating to a person who was in the community when the certificate was granted?

20 No, the statutory procedures with respect to the granting of the certificate are the same. It should be remembered, however, that a hospital in-patient may only be detained on the authority of a short-term detention certificate for a *total* of 28 days. The 2-stage process of 3 days for the patient's removal to hospital followed by 28 days of hospitalisation does not apply where a short-term detention certificate is granted with respect to a hospital in-patient.

21 For a discussion of issues relating to the subject of unlawful detention with respect to informal patients, please see Chapter 7 of Volume 1 of the Code of Practice.

chapter two

Process preceding the granting of the short-term detention certificate

Which criteria must be met before the short-term detention certificate can be granted?

22 The approved medical practitioner must consider it likely that the criteria which are listed at section 44(4) of the Act have been met before a short-term detention certificate can be granted. The criteria are that:

- the patient has a mental disorder;
- because of the mental disorder, the patient's ability to make decisions about the provision of medical treatment is significantly impaired;
- it is necessary to detain the patient in hospital for the purpose of determining what medical treatment should be given to the patient or giving medical treatment to the patient;
- if the patient were not detained in hospital there would be a significant risk to the health, safety or welfare of the patient or to the safety of any other person; and
- the granting of a short-term detention certificate is necessary.

23 It should be noted that these conditions are cumulative: that is, that all five conditions must be met before the short-term detention certificate can be granted.

24 In instances where the practitioner believes that the patient will not undergo treatment voluntarily during the detention period even if the patient claims to consent to treatment before or at the beginning of the detention period, the practitioner should use his/her judgement to decide whether the patient's claim can be relied upon. This requires a close examination of the person's previous psychiatric history and also as full and proper a consultation between the medical practitioners, the MHO and relevant other parties providing care and treatment to the patient as patient confidentiality allows.

What form of medical examination should the medical practitioner carry out before granting a short-term detention certificate?

25 In deciding which form of medical examination is appropriate, it is important to remember that the period of detention authorised by a short-term detention certificate is longer than that authorised by an emergency detention certificate. Moreover, a short-term detention

certificate authorises the patient's detention in hospital for the dual purpose of determining what medical treatment needs to be given to the patient as well as for the giving of medical treatment for mental disorder under Part 16 of the Act. This is in contrast to an emergency detention certificate which only authorises the patient's detention in hospital for the purpose of determining what medical treatment needs to be given. It would therefore be expected that the medical practitioner would carry out a sufficiently thorough examination of the patient to justify this longer period of detention and the giving of medical treatment authorised by a short-term detention certificate.

26 It would be expected then that an examination would always include:

- a direct, face-to-face, personal examination of the patient;
- a mental state examination;
- an assessment of the patient's decision-making ability and of whether the patient will agree to treatment on a voluntary basis;
- an assessment of the patient's physical state in order to help decide whether the patient should be sent to a psychiatric hospital receiving service or to a medical hospital receiving service;
- an assessment of the potential risk to the patient and/or others; and
- consideration of as much available and relevant information on the patient's medical and social circumstances as is possible under the circumstances of an emergency, including, where available and practicable, what is contained in past records, case notes as well as the views of carers and any other parties who may be providing care and treatment to the patient.

27 Where the patient will not consent to being examined, the medical practitioner should weigh up whatever information is available in the context of the patient's current presentation, their past psychiatric history and the views of other members of the multi-disciplinary team to make a pragmatic decision balancing the right of the patient to treatment with the need to provide such treatment in the least restrictive environment. It may well be that an emergency detention certificate would be the most appropriate detention authority to grant in such cases, assuming that the relevant detention criteria are met.

28 It should be noted that section 44 of the Act provides that the short-term detention certificate must be granted within 3 days of the completion of the initial medical examination.

chapter two

Which other steps must the approved medical practitioner take before the certificate can be granted?

29 The Act imposes two specific duties on the approved medical practitioner. These are:

- to consult and obtain the consent of an MHO to the granting of the certificate; and
- to consult and have regard to the views of the patient's named person, where it is practicable to do so.

30 The first duty is to consult an MHO with regard to the granting of a short-term detention certificate. The certificate can only be granted if that MHO has granted his/her consent. It would be expected that a medical practitioner would not 'shop around' for an MHO who will consent to the granting of the detention certificate where one MHO has already refused consent. However, to account for a highly exceptional circumstance in which a medical practitioner wishes to seek a second MHO opinion, it will be important for the procedures for and the circumstances in which such a second opinion may be sought to be set out in agreed protocols between the local authority and the relevant health partners. In any case where a second MHO assessment is sought, the second MHO should always be informed that another MHO has already refused consent to the granting of the certificate and of the reasons for this refusal.

31 The second duty is to consult the patient's named person and have regard to their views with respect to the proposed detention certificate, where this is practicable to do so. A medical practitioner will need to remember that the Act places a duty on the MHO to ascertain the name and address of the named person. *(For further details on this point see paragraphs 45 and 51 of this Chapter.)* The MHO should pass these details to the approved medical practitioner as quickly as possible within the detention process to enable the approved medical practitioner to comply with this duty of consultation.

32 Where it has not been practicable for the approved medical practitioner to consult the named person in advance of granting the certificate, it would be best practice for him/her to attempt to consult the named person as soon as practicably possible after the certificate has been granted.

33 In considering whether or not it would be appropriate to grant a short-term detention certificate, the approved medical practitioner should take into account relevant information from the other members of the multi-disciplinary team who are providing care and treatment to the patient. The MHO and AMP should also remember that section 1(3) of the Act imposes on them a duty to have regard to the views of the present and past wishes and feelings of the patient which are relevant to the situation and to the views of the patient's named person, any carer, guardian and welfare attorney of the patient.

Which steps must be taken by the MHO before consenting to the granting of the certificate?

34 Before the MHO can come to a conclusion on whether or not to consent to the granting of the short-term detention certificate, he/she will need, wherever practicable, to try to elicit the views of the patient with respect to the proposed detention and to any alternative courses of action. The MHO will then need to elicit relevant information about the patient's personal and social circumstances from other mental health professionals who have knowledge of the patient. This could involve a discussion with the medical practitioner about his/her views on why a period of detention is appropriate; what he/she has observed; why he/she feels that the person's health, safety or welfare or the safety of others is at significant risk as a result of the mental disorder; and why any delay in having recourse to a short-term detention certificate would be undesirable. It will also be important to seek information on such issues from other sources where they are available and where this proves to be practicable. These other sources could include the patient's named person, where the patient already has one, or carers/relatives. Any advance statement, where one exists, should also be considered. All such information will be of relevance not only to the MHO in his/her decision about granting consent but also to the practitioner who is considering whether or not to grant the certificate.

35 Once the MHO is in possession of as much of the above information as is possible and practicable in the circumstances, he/she will need to assess any possible alternatives to the proposed period of formal detention in hospital. He/she should therefore make sure that as many forms of informal and less restrictive treatment as practicable have been explored before consenting to the last resort of compulsory detention.

chapter two

36 An important consideration for the MHO in deciding whether or not to consent to the granting of the certificate is the likely impact on the person and their carers/family of the detention *not* taking place. The MHO will therefore need to give serious consideration to whether the patient's family/carers, etc are willing and able to continue to care for and support the patient in an appropriate manner, if they have already been involved in doing so, and, if not, whether alternative forms of community-based care and support is appropriate and available.

37 It would be expected that, where practicable, if the patient has been in receipt of mental health services prior to the certificate being granted, members of the multi-disciplinary team providing those services would be consulted. This will be particularly important where the patient was immediately beforehand subject to an emergency detention certificate. These parties may be able to provide knowledge of the possible and viable alternatives to compulsory powers and may also need to be involved in planning the patient's care and treatment if the detention certificate is ultimately granted.

38 In essence, the MHO should be taking into account the following questions when deciding whether to consent to the granting of the short-term detention certificate:

- do you believe, after appropriate assessment, that all the detention criteria have been met?
- do you believe that the principles of the Act (see sections 1 and 2 of the Act) have been adhered to in both letter and spirit? For example, have all relevant, less restrictive alternatives been considered?
- is there strong reliable evidence that the patient's treatment could be provided on a voluntary basis? Do you believe that recourse to compulsory measures could be avoided whilst protecting the patient's rights?
- are you and the approved medical practitioner in possession of sufficient information on which to base a sound professional judgement?

39 In order to be in a position to answer the questions above, the MHO must comply with a series of duties. These duties are outlined in section 45 of the Act. The MHO must:

- interview the patient;
- ascertain the name and address of the patient's named person; and
- inform the patient of the availability of independent advocacy services; and

- take appropriate steps to ensure that the patient has the opportunity to make use of these advocacy services.

These three areas are dealt with in paragraphs 41 to 54 of this chapter.

40 In circumstances where it is impractical for the MHO to interview the patient or to ascertain the name and address of the patient's named person, the MHO must record the steps taken with a view to complying with the duties, and before the expiry of 7 days beginning with the day the MHO was consulted, give a copy of that record to the AMP.

The MHO's interview with the patient

41 During the interview, the MHO should explain to the patient what a period of short-term detention can involve in the event of the certificate being granted. The MHO should also attempt to learn the patient's views on his/her circumstances, his/her attitude towards the assessment of mental disorder and the proposed treatment (where this is known) and the proposed hospitalisation. It would also be good practice to provide the patient with an explanation of his/her right to appeal to the Tribunal and with advice on how to access legal support as well as the support of an independent advocate in the event of the detention certificate being granted.

42 There are only a small number of circumstances in which the MHO might consider consenting to the granting of the certificate without, at the very least, having been in the physical presence of the patient. Circumstances which would not preclude the MHO giving his/her consent to the certificate being granted without having interviewed the patient could include:

- where communication difficulties with the patient cannot be overcome speedily; and
- where the patient is extremely dangerous or violent; and
- where the patient refuses to co-operate or participate in the interview.

43 Even under such circumstances, it would be expected that the MHO would elicit as much information as possible about the proposed detention from the patient's family, friends, carers, GP, psychiatric nurse, advance statements, social work records in advance of granting his/her consent to the detention certificate. Similarly, it may well be best for the MHO to defer his/her decision with respect to consenting to the granting of the certificate until the patient can be interviewed in more favourable circumstances.

chapter two

44 There may be other exceptional circumstances (such as a ferry strike, etc) which would prevent the MHO from interviewing the patient. Given that such circumstances are by their nature exceptional and given that standard practice routinely includes a face-to-face MHO assessment, it would be appropriate for consent to be given where the MHO is satisfied that the approved medical practitioner's assessment is based on the fullest set of information available. It would be best practice for the MHO, however, to ensure that he/she undertakes an assessment of the patient as soon as is possible after the certificate has been granted and to make available to the hospital managers, the relevant local authority/authorities and the Commission a full account of the exceptional circumstances which led to the MHO consenting to the certificate without interviewing the patient.

45 If an MHO refuses to consent to the granting of a short-term detention certificate (assuming that he/she has had an opportunity to assess the patient), it would not be acceptable for that medical practitioner to grant an emergency detention certificate instead (for which the consent of the MHO is not mandatory), unless the patient's clinical situation has changed in the interim. However, the MHO would still need to be able to justify his/her refusal to consent to the detention against the opinion of the approved medical practitioner. Many of the duties which an MHO would be expected to carry out subsequent to a refusal to consent to the granting of an emergency detention certificate apply to a refusal to consent to the granting of a short-term detention certificate (see Chapter 7 of this Volume). In particular, it would be best practice for the MHO to submit a justification of his/her refusal to the MWC and the RMO and for that to be included in the patient's medical notes. Rather than refuse consent to the certificate outright, one option might be for the MHO to encourage the practitioner to defer making a firm decision on the need to grant the certificate until the MHO has had the full opportunity to contribute to the joint assessment process. The short-term detention certificate can, after all, be granted up to 3 days after the initial medical examination has taken place.

Ascertaining the name and address of the patient's named person

46 Section 45(1)(b) of the Act states that the MHO must ascertain the name and address of the patient's named person before deciding whether to consent to the granting of the short-term detention certificate. Identifying the patient's named person may necessitate discussion with the medical

practitioner who is considering granting the detention certificate and/or other relevant professionals as to whether the patient has the capacity to nominate a named person.

47 It would be best practice for the MHO to first explain to the patient verbally and with a follow-up leaflet, the status and rights of the named person with respect to the short-term detention certificate as well as the role they can play in the CTO application process and beyond. The MHO will consequently also need to explain the difference between the roles of the named person and the independent advocate.

48 An MHO will need to be very familiar with the procedures outlined in Part 17 Chapter 1 of the Act regarding the nomination process of the named person. This is because under section 255 of the Act the MHO has a duty in certain circumstances and a power at other times to apply to the Tribunal for an order under section 257 to remove and replace an "apparent named person" (i.e. a person whom the MHO has deemed to be inappropriate to act in that role). The decision as to whether or not the apparent named person is inappropriate to act should not be made by the MHO alone but in consultation with other relevant parties of the patient's multi-disciplinary team. The expectation is that the patient's right to choose whom he/she wishes to have as a named person would be respected. The MHO has no power to veto the patient's choice at the time of nomination, nor should they apply undue influence on the patient. The MHO should intervene using the powers given at section 255 only where there are clear and significant reasons for doing so. *(For further information regarding the nomination process of a named person, see Part 17 Chapter 1 of the Act or Chapter 2 of Volume 1 of the Code of Practice.)*

49 The MHO should explain to the patient that in the absence of them nominating a named person, their primary carer shall become their named person. When ascertaining the identity of the named person and the primary carer, the MHO should be careful to balance the patient's rights with respect to confidentiality (the patient may wish, for example, a relative with whom they have a poor or abusive relationship to know little about their detention) with the need for the MHO to be in possession of sufficient information on which to make an informed decision.

50 As with all occasions where a named person is being nominated, the MHO should consider the impact on the nearest relative/primary carer where they are not nominated as the named person. This could be done by explaining to them the role of the named person and the rights of relatives or carers who are not nominated as the patient's named person.

51 The MHO should make sure that the named person is fully aware of the fact that they have been nominated; of the fact that he/she is indeed willing to act as the named person; what the role of named person entails; and what rights and responsibilities it confers on them, for example, in relation to making an application to the Tribunal to revoke a short-term detention certificate. It would also be best practice for the MHO to ascertain at this stage whether the patient has an advance statement and, where one exists, to convey information on its existence and contents to the relevant parties providing the patient with medical treatment.

Informing the patient of independent advocacy rights

52 The MHO should provide an explanation to the patient of the role of an independent advocate and of how an independent advocate might be able to help them both now and in the future. Wherever possible, this should be done in person. The MHO should also make this information available in printed form in appropriate languages/format, etc. As with any process of information giving, this should be a dynamic process with an ongoing assessment of the patient's capacity to understand and retain the information. Merely handing a leaflet to the patient is unlikely to be considered as acceptable in terms of the MHO fulfilling their duties. It may be acceptable, however, if all other options have been tried and have failed. Overall, the MHO may be assisted in carrying out these duties by other members of the multi-disciplinary team involved in the patient's care and treatment.

53 The MHO will also need to play a part in ensuring that hospital ward staff (if the patient is ultimately detained) are aware of the extent of the independent advocate's involvement in that patient's case. The MHO will want to monitor effective access to independent advocacy services and to intervene more actively where problems arise.

54 It should be noted that section 260(2)(a)(iii) places a duty on hospital managers to inform the patient, subsequent to a range of events taking place, of the availability of independent advocacy services and to take appropriate steps to ensure that the patient has the opportunity to make use of those services. One such event is the granting of a short-term detention certificate.

When must the certificate be completed and what might it look like?

55 Section 44(1) states that the approved medical practitioner who examined the patient must grant the certificate. It cannot be completed by anyone else. The detention certificate must be granted within 3 days of completing the medical examination. (There is no form prescribed for these treatments but a pro-forma, DET2, may be found on the Scottish Executive website at: www.scotland.gov.uk/health.mentalhealthlaw.)

56 Section 44(9) states that the certificate must state the reasons for believing the criteria for granting the certificate to be met. The medical practitioner should give specific reasons on the detention certificate for why he/she believes *each* of the conditions are met. One 'blanket' reason should not be given to cover all the criteria. The medical practitioner must sign the certificate.

Process following the granting of the short-term detention certificate

Transferring and admitting the patient to hospital

57 Where a short-term detention certificate is granted in respect of a person who was not a hospital in-patient when the certificate was granted, many of the same problems and issues will arise with respect to that person's transfer and admission to hospital as arise in relation to the transfer and admission of a person subject to an emergency detention certificate. *For further information on this subject and on psychiatric emergency plans, please see Chapter 7 of this Volume of the Code of Practice.*

What should the medical practitioner who granted the certificate do after it has been granted?

58 Where that practitioner is to have no further involvement with the patient's care and treatment, the only duty on that medical practitioner is to ensure that the detention certificate is passed to the managers of the hospital in which the patient is to be detained. Section 44 makes clear that the patient's detention in hospital is only authorised if the certificate has been given to the hospital managers before the patient is admitted. The actual person(s) in an individual hospital who may perform the function of receiving the certificate on behalf of the hospital managers should be clearly designated and identified by those managers.

What should the MHO do once the certificate has been granted?

59 The MHO must prepare a social circumstances report within 21 days of the short-term detention certificate being granted, unless he/she is satisfied that such a report would serve little or no practical purpose. *For further information on social circumstances reports, see Chapter 11 of Volume 1 of this Code of Practice.*

60 Best practice would suggest that the MHO should consider whether the following are appropriate:

- ensuring that the patient is as aware as is possible of his/her status and rights and has access to information on representation, advocacy services, and interpretation or translation services;
- consulting the patient's carers and eliciting their views;
- attending the ward assessment meeting and liaising with ward staff and other members of the multi-disciplinary team, particularly where the patient was using mental health services prior to being hospitalised;
- ensuring that ward medical staff are aware of the patient's views on consent to treatment, including the existence and content of any advance statement made by the patient;
- ensuring that a written record of the MHO's decision to give consent is included in the patient's records;
- liaising with community care teams, other sections of the local authority (Criminal Justice Teams, CMHT, Housing, Education, Leisure and Recreation, etc) and other relevant statutory and non-statutory organisations (e.g. supported accommodation or visiting support workers) for the purposes of through-care planning, wherever necessary;
- ensuring that any dependants which the patient might have are being appropriately cared for, particularly where there may be children or other vulnerable persons previously in the charge of the patient;
- securing the patient's property and belongings, if necessary, and arranging, for example, suitable pet care;
- determining whether a full community care assessment should be undertaken under section 227 of the Act and make such a request to the local authority if they are not going to be undertaking this assessment themselves;
- beginning preparations for any eventual CTO application or for a discharge plan of care;
- attending to issues which the patient may face in relation to their personal finances (e.g. benefits, employment, etc) because of their detention in hospital;
- making sure that the patient and the named person, etc remain fully aware of their rights throughout the detention period – for example, in relation to their right to appeal for a revocation of the short-term detention certificate under section 50 or in relation to their rights to advocacy services.

chapter two

What duties are placed on hospital managers with respect to a short-term detention certificate?

61 The Act places a range of duties on the managers of the hospital to which the patient has been admitted when subject to a short-term detention certificate. These duties are set out in paragraphs 64 to 65.

62 Section 46 places a duty on hospital managers to notify certain parties of the granting of the short-term detention certificate as soon as is practicable after they have received the certificate. The parties are:

- the patient;
- the patient's named person;
- any guardian of the patient under the 2000 Act; and
- any welfare attorney of the patient under the 2000 Act.

63 Within 7 days of the certificate being granted, hospital managers must also notify the Tribunal and the Commission that the certificate has been granted. They must also send them a copy of the detention certificate. Best practice would suggest that the patient's named person, guardian, etc, be informed orally first (for example, by telephone) rather than have to wait for the formal written notification to arrive in the post several days after the detention has taken place.

64 Section 260 of the Act places a duty on the managers of the hospital to which the patient is admitted to provide the patient with a range of information which principally relates to the patient's rights. Section 261 similarly places duties on those hospital managers to provide the patient with assistance in overcoming communications problems.

65 Finally, section 230 obliges hospital managers to appoint an approved medical practitioner to act as the patient's responsible medical officer as soon as is practicable after the granting of the short-term detention certificate. Acute medical and surgical hospital management services will need to enter into local arrangements with psychiatric providers to ensure the availability of approved medical practitioners to act as the RMO for such a patient. *(For further information on this, see Chapter 9 of Volume 1 of the Code of Practice.)* Where it is practicable, it would be best practice for the approved medical practitioner appointed as the patient's RMO to be the same practitioner who examined the patient as soon as practicable after admission to hospital.

Which forms of treatment can be given to a patient subject to a short-term detention certificate?

66 Section 44(5) states that the patient can be given medical treatment for their mental disorder under Part 16 of the Act. *For a discussion of the definition of medical treatment set out in the Act, see Chapter 1 of Volume 1 of the Code of Practice.*

chapter two

Revoking a short-term detention certificate

67 There are 3 ways in which a short-term detention certificate can be revoked, and these are described in paragraphs 68 to 78 of this chapter. The 3 ways are:
- by the patient's RMO;
- by the Tribunal subsequent to an application under section 50 by the patient or the patient's named person; and
- by the Commission.

Review and revocation of short-term detention certificate by RMO

68 Section 49 places a duty on the patient's RMO to keep under the review the continued necessity for the short-term detention certificate. If the RMO is satisfied that the patient no longer meets the detention criteria listed in section 49(1) of the Act or that the continued detention of the patient in hospital is no longer necessary, then the RMO must revoke the detention certificate. Where the RMO does revoke a certificate, he/she must as soon as is practicable give written notice of the revocation to the following parties:
- the patient;
- the patient's named person;
- any guardian of the patient;
- any welfare attorney of the patient; and
- the MHO who consented to the granting of the detention certificate.

69 The RMO must also give written notice to the Tribunal and the Commission within 7 days of the certificate being revoked. Best practice dictates that the patient and the parties listed at the paragraph above also be informed orally of the revocation of the detention certificate immediately. Close consideration should also be given to the actions required to meet any support needs as part of the discharge plan of care.

70 Although the RMO is under a duty to review the certificate "from time to time", best practice would suggest that the RMO keep the need for the certificate under continual review. In practical terms, this could mean carrying out an at least weekly review with input into the decision-making process from the full multi-disciplinary team involved with the patient's care. Moreover, all ward staff should remain active in this review process, and it will be vitally important that the RMO seeks the views of other members of the multi-disciplinary team, particularly from the patient's MHO, before taking the decision to revoke the certificate.

71 Note that the medical practitioner acting as the patient's RMO is the only practitioner who can revoke a short-term detention certificate.

The patient's and the patient's named person's right to apply to the Tribunal for a revocation of the short-term detention certificate

72 Section 50 confers on the patient and the patient's named person the right to appeal to the Tribunal where the patient is subject to a short-term detention certificate. Before the Tribunal makes a decision on the appeal, it must allow the following parties the chance to make representations orally or in writing and to lead or produce evidence:

- the patient;
- the patient's named person;
- any guardian of the patient;
- any welfare attorney of the patient;
- the approved medical practitioner who granted the certificate;
- the MHO who consented to the granting of the certificate;
- the patient's RMO;
- any *curator ad litem* appointed by the Tribunal; and
- any other person who appears to the Tribunal to have an interest in the application (for example, the patient's nearest relative (if they are not the primary carer), solicitor, other medical practitioner or clinical psychologist they wish to call to give evidence, etc).

73 In determining the appeal, the Tribunal must judge whether the criteria listed at section 50(4) continue to be met. The criteria are:

- that the patient has a mental disorder;
- that, because of that mental disorder, the patient's ability to make decisions about the provision of medical treatment for that mental disorder is significantly impaired; and
- that there would be a significant risk to the health, safety or welfare of the patient or to the safety of any other person if the patient were not detained in hospital.

74 If these criteria do not continue to be met, or if the Tribunal is not satisfied that it continues to be necessary for the patient's detention in hospital to be authorised by the short-term detention certificate, then the Tribunal must revoke the certificate.

75 It should be noted that the onus does not rest on the patient (or the patient's representatives) to demonstrate that the patient does not require to be subject to the compulsory powers authorised by the certificate. Instead, evidence justifying the continuing recourse to compulsory powers will have to come from a range of sources, including the patient's RMO (if one has been appointed), the medical practitioner who granted the certificate, and other members of the multi-disciplinary team providing care and treatment to the patient.

The Commission can revoke the certificate

76 Section 51 of the Act confers on the Commission a power to revoke a short-term detention certificate where it is not satisfied that the following conditions continue to be met:

- that the patient has a mental disorder;
- that, because of that mental disorder, the patient's ability to make decisions about the provision of medical treatment for that mental disorder is significantly impaired; and
- that there would be a significant risk to the health, safety or welfare of the patient or to the safety of any other person if the patient were not detained in hospital.

77 The Commission may also revoke the short-term detention certificate where it is satisfied that it is no longer necessary for the patient to be detained in hospital on the authority of the certificate.

78 Where the Commission revokes a certificate under these circumstances, it must notify in writing the following parties as soon as is practicable after revoking the certificate:

- the patient;
- the patient's named person;
- any guardian of the patient;
- any welfare attorney of the patient;
- the managers of the hospital in which the patient is detained;
- the MHO who consented to the granting of the certificate; and
- the Tribunal.

chapter two

Extending a period of short-term detention

79 There are two ways in which a period of short-term detention can be extended. These are:

- the granting of an extension certificate under section 47 of the Act; and
- where a CTO has been submitted to the Tribunal.

Granting an "extension certificate"

80 The first way in which a period of short-term detention can be extended is by the granting of an "extension certificate" under sections 47 and 48 of the Act. This is a detention certificate which authorises the patient's continued detention in hospital for a period of 3 working days beginning with the expiry of the short-term detention certificate. It also authorises the giving of medical treatment to the patient in accordance with Part 16 of the Act. The purpose of an extension certificate is to extend the patient's detention in hospital in order to enable an application for a compulsory treatment order to be prepared.

81 An extension certificate may only be granted by an approved medical practitioner in terms of section 47(1) of the Act. It should be noted that the certificate must be granted within the period of 24 hours beginning with the completion of the medical examination. Where an extension certificate is granted, it is recommended that form is always used.

When may an extension certificate be granted?

82 The power to grant an extension certificate should only be exercised where there has been a change in the patient's health in the days immediately prior to the expiry of the short-term detention certificate with the result that there would be insufficient time to put together an application for a compulsory treatment order. The criteria which must be met before this extension certificate can be granted are:

- that the patient has a mental disorder;
- that, because of the mental disorder, the patient's ability to make decisions about the medical treatment to be provided for that mental disorder is significantly impaired;
- that it is necessary to detain the patient in hospital for the purpose of determining what medical treatment should be given or of giving medical treatment to the patient;

- that there would be a significant risk to the health, safety or welfare of the patient or to the safety of another person if the patient were not detained in hospital; and
- that because of a change in the mental health of the patient, an application for a CTO should be made.

83 These detention criteria are very similar to those which must be met before a short-term detention certificate can be granted. Note, however, that section 47(2)(b) of the Act states that the approved medical practitioner *must consider these criteria to be met*. This compares with the detention criteria for a short-term detention certificate where the RMO need only consider that the relevant detention criteria *are likely* to be met (see section 44(3)(b) of the Act).

84 It would be best practice to ensure that, where practicable, the extension certificate be granted by the patient's RMO rather than a different approved medical practitioner who has had little contact with the patient during the period of detention authorised by the period of short-term detention. The approved medical practitioner who examines the patient prior to the granting of the extension certificate should also ensure that there is no conflict of interest in relation to the medical examination.

Conflict of interest with respect to the granting of an extension certificate

85 Section 47(2)(a) of the Act stipulates that an extension certificate may only be granted where there is no conflict of interest in relation to the medical examination. Section 47(5) provides for a regulation-making power to specify the circumstances in which there is and there is not be taken to be such a conflict of interest. **The Mental Health (Care and Treatment) (Conflict of Interest) (No 2) (Scotland) Regulations 2005** apply when granting an extension certificate as when granting a short-term detention certificate. See paragraph 13 of this chapter for details.

Must an MHO be consulted in advance of the extension certificate being granted?

86 Yes. An MHO should be consulted and his/her consent sought, wherever practicable, before the practitioner can grant an extension certificate. The Act states that the consent of *an* MHO is required before the certificate can be granted, where this is practicable. This means that the practitioner may seek the consent of *any* MHO rather than the consent of the designated MHO. However, it would always be best practice to make every effort to involve the designated MHO to ensure continuity and consistency in the assessment process.

Who must be notified that an extension certificate has been granted?

87 Within 24 hours of the extension certificate being granted, the approved medical practitioner must give the extension certificate to the managers of the hospital in which the patient is to be detained. That practitioner must also provide notification of the granting of the extension certificate to the following parties:

- the patient;
- the patient's named person;
- the Tribunal;
- the Commission;
- any guardian of the patient;
- any welfare attorney of the patient; and
- the patient's MHO.

88 The parties listed in the previous paragraph must also be notified of a range of other issues connected to the granting of the certificate under section 48(1) of the Act. These are:

- the approved medical practitioner's reasons for believing that the patient met the detention criteria listed at section 44(4)(a) to (d) of the Act (that is, the conditions described in paragraph 84 above);
- whether the consent of an MHO was obtained to the granting of the extension certificate; and
- if the consent of an MHO was not obtained prior to the extension certificate being granted, the reason why it was impracticable to consult an MHO.

89 The practitioner should consider whether the parties listed at paragraph 89 above should be informed verbally first as if notification is sent out in the post, it is unlikely to be received within 24 hours.

Can an extension certificate be revoked? Is there an appeal procedure against an extension certificate?

90 Yes. The appeal and revocation procedures with respect to extension certificates are the same as those relating to a short-term detention certificate. For further information on these procedures, see paragraphs 68 to 71 and 72 to 78 of this chapter, respectively.

Extending the short-term detention period pending the outcome of a CTO application

91 The second way in which a period of short-term detention can be extended is where a CTO application has been submitted to the Tribunal. Section 68 of the Act states that once an application for a CTO has been submitted to the Tribunal, the patient's detention in hospital continues to be authorised for a further 5 working days from the point where the short-term detention certificate or extension certificate would have expired.

Interaction of short-term detention certificates with other detention certificates

92 Section 55 of the Act states that any emergency detention certificate must be revoked once the short-term detention certificate has been granted. Section 56 of the Act provides that where a patient is subject to a compulsory treatment order and a short-term detention certificate is granted in respect of that patient, the measures authorised in the CTO cease to be authorised for the period of the short-term detention certificate.

93 It would be best practice to ensure that the notifications of both the detention and its subsequent revocation have been made as required by the Act.

Suspending a short-term detention certificate (sections 53 and 54)

94 Where a patient is subject to a short-term detention certificate and is detained in hospital on the authority of that certificate, it is possible to suspend that certificate for a limited period of time (and thereby suspend the patient's detention in hospital) without revoking the certificate in its entirety. Under such circumstances, section 53 of the Act allows for a "suspension certificate" to be granted. Such a certificate can only be granted by the patient's RMO.

How long does a suspension certificate last?

95 A suspension certificate can last for any period of time stipulated by the patient's RMO. In terms of section 53(2), this period specified in the suspension certificate may be the duration of an event or series of events with or without any associated travel. By implication, the time and date on which this suspension certificate is due to expire may not go beyond the time and date on which the short-term detention certificate is due to expire.

Can conditions be attached to the suspension certificate?

96 Yes. The patient's RMO may attach conditions to this suspension certificate. In terms of section 53(4) of the Act, such conditions are that:

- the patient be kept in the charge of a person authorised in writing for that purpose by the patient's RMO for the period specified in the certificate; and
- any other conditions which the patient's RMO wishes to specify.

97 The patient's RMO can only grant such conditions where, in terms of section 53(3) of the Act, he/she considers them to be in the interests of the patient or necessary for the protection of any other person. It should be noted that the RMO's giving of authority to another person to keep a patient in his/her charge can only be done in writing.

98 Examples of conditions which could be attached to a suspension certificate include that the patient live in a specified place under the care of a specified person; be kept in the charge of an escorting nurse; or that the patient accept visits from a medical practitioner or an MHO. It would be best practice for the RMO to ensure that the patient's MHO and other members of the multi-disciplinary team are informed of any

conditions attached to the suspension certificate, and to ensure that procedures and contingency plans are put in place for any occasion where the conditions are not complied with.

When would it be appropriate to grant a suspension certificate?

99 The range of events and occurrences which might give rise to the granting under section 53 of a suspension certificate is likely to be greater than that which might give rise to the granting of a suspension certificate under section 41 of the Act suspending an emergency detention certificate. It may be necessary to suspend the short-term detention certificate in order to plan discharge and care planning: for example, to allow the patient to visit and/or be assessed by a community care service provider; or to allow the patient to be gradually re-integrated into their pre-existing social circumstances in the community, including making visits and staying overnight at home, with relatives and carers, or in other care facilities. Before any decision is taken with respect to granting a suspension certificate, however, it would be expected that the patient's RMO consult with the MHO and other members of the multi-disciplinary team. The potential risk to the health and welfare of the patient and of others should be assessed as well as the extent to which the proposed suspension period will aid the patient's recovery. Practitioners are also reminded that they should have regard to the matters laid out in sections 1 to 3 of the Act, when deciding whether or not to grant a suspension certificate.

100 A suspension certificate should not be granted under section 53 of the Act as a means of managing beds in wards which are running at or above capacity. A decision to suspend the power to detain the patient in hospital should only ever be taken where it is in the best interests of the patient.

Who is responsible for the patient's care and treatment while subject to a suspension certificate?

101 The patient's RMO remains responsible for the patient's care and treatment while the patient is subject to a suspension certificate. He/she must therefore ensure that appropriate arrangements are made for the patient's care and treatment while not in hospital. It should also be remembered that the duty under section 1(6) of the Act to provide "appropriate services" to the patient includes any time where the patient is subject to a suspension certificate.

102 It is important that the patient's relatives and/or carers (especially where the patient is residing with them for the duration of the suspension certificate) and all the members of the patient's multi-disciplinary team should have easy access to the RMO so that the patient's progress towards recovery can be effectively monitored and acted upon, where appropriate.

What should happen where a patient requires emergency treatment in another hospital?

103 There may be occasions where a patient who is detained in hospital on the authority of a short-term detention certificate requires to be transferred urgently to another hospital to receive emergency treatment for a physical disorder. A suspension certificate would not have to be granted under such circumstances as no hospital is specified in a short-term detention certificate. Best practice would suggest, however, that the RMO should take steps to ensure that the patient's named person, primary carer, MHO and other relevant members of the multi-disciplinary team are informed of any emergency transfer as soon as possible after it becomes apparent that the transfer may be necessary.

Can a suspension certificate be revoked?

104 Yes. There may be occasions where it is necessary for the patient's RMO to revoke a certificate suspending a short-term detention certificate. In accordance with section 54(2) of the Act, he/she may do this where he/she is satisfied that it is necessary in the interests of the patient to do so or that it is necessary for the protection of any other person to do so.

105 Where an RMO revokes a suspension certificate, he/she must in terms of section 54(3) of the Act notify in writing a range of parties of the revocation as soon as practicable after it has taken place. These parties are:

- the patient;
- the patient's named person;
- the patient's MHO;
- any person who had been authorised by the RMO to keep the patient in his/her charge for the duration of the suspension certificate; and
- the Commission.

(There is no form prescribed for these treatments but a pro-forma, REV1, may be found on the Scottish Executive website at: www.scotland.gov.uk/health.mentalhealthlaw.)

Guide for medical practitioners on the granting of a short-term detention certificate under section 44 of the Mental Health (Care and Treatment) (Scotland) Act 2003

Approved medical practitioner (AMP) (see note 1) carries out a medical examination and recommends hospital admission.

Patient Refuses Admission

Consider the following grounds for detention:

1. You consider it likely that conditions (a) to (e) are met:
(a) the patient has a mental disorder (see note 2);
(b) because of that mental disorder, the patient's ability to make decisions about the provision of medical treatment for that mental disorder is significantly impaired;
(c) it is necessary to detain the patient in hospital for the purpose of determining what medical treatment requires to be provided to the patient or of giving medical treatment to the patient;
(d) there would be a significant risk to the health, safety or welfare of the patient or to the safety of any other person if he/she were not detained in hospital;
(e) the granting of a short-term detention certificate is necessary.
AND
2. Immediately before the medical examination, the patient was not detained in hospital by way of certain provisions of the Act (see note 3).
AND
3. There was no conflict of interest in relation to the medical examination (see note 4).

Patient Agrees to Admission

Patient subsequently decides to leave.

Continue hospital treatment.

AMP available to examine patient. → Consider whether criteria for a short-term detention certificate are met.

Non-AMP available to examine patient. → Consider whether criteria for an emergency detention certificate are met.

No medical practitioner available. → Consider using nurse's holding power under section 299.

All the above detention criteria are met.

All the detention criteria above are not met: a short-term detention certificate may not be granted.

You must consult a mental health officer (MHO) and obtain their consent to the granting of the certificate. If that consent is not given, you may not grant the short-term detention certificate.

You must, where practicable, consult the patient's named person before granting the certificate and must have regard to the named person. See notes 5 and 6.

NEXT STEPS:
1. Inform the patient of the decision to grant the certificate.
2. Complete and sign the short-term detention certificate within prescribed timescales (see notes 7, 8 and 9).
3. Ensure that arrangements are in place for the patient's transfer to hospital, where this is required.
4. Ensure that the detention certificate is passed to the relevant hospital managers (see note 10).

Throughout the process of granting a short-term detention certificate, you must have regard to the principles of the legislation in section 1 and the other matters laid out in sections 2 and 3 of the Act.

Note 1: Only an approved medical practitioner may grant a short-term detention certificate (i.e. a medical practitioner approved under section 22 of the Act).

Note 2: Section 328(1) of the Act defines "mental disorder" as "mental illness, personality disorder or learning disability, however not by reason only of sexual orientation; sexual deviancy; trans-sexualism; transvestism; dependence on, or use of alcohol or drugs; behaviour that causes, or is likely to cause, harassment, alarm or distress to any other person; or acting as no prudent person would act".

Note 3: The relevant provisions are set out at section 44(2) of the Act. They are:

- a short-term detention certificate;
- an extension certificate issued under section 47 of the Act pending an application for a CTO;
- section 68 of the Act (i.e. the extension to the detention period authorised once a CTO application has been submitted to the Tribunal);
- a certificate granted under sections 114(2) or 115(2) of the Act (i.e. a certificate issued subsequent to a patient's non-compliance with the terms of a community-based interim CTO or a CTO).

Note 4: Regulations prescribe the circumstances where there is and there is not to be taken a conflict of interest in relation to the medical examination of a patient subject to short-term detention in hospital and a CTO. The Regulations also list the prohibited degrees of relationship. For further information on conflict of interest, see Chapter 4 of this Volume of the Code of Practice.

Note 5: A short-term detention certificate can only be granted if you have consulted the patient's named person about the proposed granting of the certificate, where it was practicable to do so, and if you have had regard to their views.

Note 6: You should ask the MHO whose consent you have sought to the granting of the certificate about the identity of the patient's named person. Section 45(1) of the Act places that MHO under a duty to interview the patient and to ascertain the name and address of the patient's named person before he/she consents to the granting of the certificate, where it is practicable to do so. If the MHO cannot carry out these duties, he/she must provide you within 7 days of you consulting him/her with a copy of a record which states the steps which he/she took in trying to carry out these duties.

Note 7: There is no form prescribed when granting a short-term detention certificate but it is strongly recommended you use pro forma, DET2. This pro forma may be found on the Scottish Executive website at: www.scotland.gov.uk/health/mentalhealthlaw. Where pro forma DET2 is not used, for the certificate to be valid, it must state the practitioner's reasons for believing that the grounds for detention are met and must be signed by the practitioner. (See lilac box of flow chart overleaf.)

Note 8: The short-term detention certificate must be completed within 3 days of the completion of the medical examination.

Note 9: The short-term detention certificate authorises, firstly, the patient's transfer to hospital within 3 days of the certificate being granted and, secondly, the patient's detention in hospital for 28 days.

Note 10: Section 44(6) of the Act states that the patient's detention in hospital is only authorised if the certificate is given to the managers of the hospital before the patient is admitted to hospital under the authority of the certificate. If the patient is already in hospital when the certificate is granted, then the certificate must be given to the hospital managers as soon as practicable after it was granted.

chapter 3

applying for a compulsory treatment order (part 7 chapter 1)

chapter three

Introduction

This chapter looks at the process involved in preparing an application for a compulsory treatment order (CTO) and in the determination of that application the Mental Health Tribunal for Scotland. The flowchart on page 59 provides an overview of this process.

The first section of this chapter describes the overall framework for the preparation of an application for a CTO while the second provides details about the medical recommendations which initiate the application.

The third section turns to the MHO's report and the proposed care plan which accompany the application.

Finally, the chapter discusses the various possible outcomes with respect to a CTO application.

Note that at the end of this chapter a table is included which aims to summarise the statutory duties to be carried out during the application process.

chapter three

FLOWCHART OF STATUTORY DUTIES TO BE CARRIED OUT DURING THE CTO APPLICATION PROCESS (PART 7, CHAPTER 1)

AMP: examines patient and prepares mental health report.

Patient's general practitioner or AMP: examines patient and prepares mental health report.

Mental health report must:
- state that the practitioner is satisfied that the conditions of section 57(3)(a) to (e) of the Act are met;
- state, for each of the conditions of section 57(3)(b) to (e) of the Act, the practitioner's reasons for believing that condition to be met;
- specify the type (or types) of mental disorder that the patient has;
- describe the symptoms of the mental disorder that the patient has and the ways in which these affect the patient;
- specify the compulsory measures that should, in his/her opinion, be authorised by the CTO;
- specify the date or dates on which the medical practitioner carried out the medical examination considers to be relevant;
- set out any other information that the medical practitioner considers to be relevant;
- (where the report is by an AMP), state whether notice of the application should be given to the patient and whether the patient is capable of arranging for representation with respect to the application.

For the application to proceed, at least one type of mental disorder and the same compulsory measures must be specified in both reports.

The medical practitioner must pass the mental health report to the MHO making the CTO application.

The MHO must ascertain the name and address of the patient's named person (section 59).

The MHO must notify the patient, the named person and the Commission that the application is to be made (subject to section 60(2)).

The MHO must:
- interview the patient;
- inform the patient that the application is to be made;
- inform the patient of advocacy rights and help the patient exercise those rights;
- inform the patient of his/her rights with respect to the application

The MHO must prepare proposed care plan in terms of section 62

The MHO must prepare a mental health officer's report in terms of section 61(4)

The MHO must prepare a CTO application in terms of section 63(2)(a)

The MHO must submit to the Tribunal:
- the 2 mental health reports;
- the MHO report;
- the proposed care plan;
- the covering application.

Tribunal considers application.

chapter three

Overview of the application process

Who must make the application? (section 57(1))

01 The application for a CTO can only be made by an MHO in the circumstances set out in section 57(1) to (5) (see paragraph 25 below). In those circumstances, the MHO must make the application even where he/she disagrees with the need for the CTO. It would be expected that the patient's designated MHO would make the application where this is practicable and where the patient already has a designated MHO as a result of being subject to, for example, a short-term detention certificate.

When must the application be made? (section 57(7))

02 An application for a CTO must be made within 14 days (that is, 14 calendar days and not 14 working days). This 14 day period begins with the date on which the medical practitioners examined the patient for the purpose of preparing their mental health reports. Where the medical practitioners examine the patient separately and on different days, the later of these dates marks the beginning of the 14 day period (see section 57(7) of the Act). The medical practitioners providing the mental health reports should bear in mind that the clock starts ticking on this 14 day period on the latest date of the medical examinations and not when the MHO receives the two medical reports. It is therefore imperative that the practitioners complete their mental health reports and transmit them to the MHO making the application as swiftly as possible after the medical examinations have taken place.

03 It should be stressed that an application for a CTO can be made even if the patient is not currently detained under the Act (for example, subject to a short-term detention certificate). Where a patient is in the community (that is, he/she is not detained under the Act), the timescales for the completion of the CTO application are the same as where the patient is detained under the Act.

chapter three

Identifying the need for an application

04 It is essential that the decision to proceed with a CTO application is only taken after all the relevant members of the patient's multi-disciplinary team have engaged in as much prior discussion as is practicable of the need for the application. It will also be essential to have regard to the views of the patient and the patient's carers and named person. Best practice is that the decision to proceed with an application should be taken after a multi-disciplinary case conference involving all relevant parties. Such parties could include CPNs, clinical psychologists, occupational therapists, the patient's advocate, relatives and/or carers, etc.

05 It would be expected that the medical practitioners providing the mental health reports contact and consult the relevant MHO service well in advance of a decision to initiate an application. This is important because the patient may have a designated MHO if he/she is already subject to, for example, a short-term detention certificate. That MHO may well be in the process of preparing a social circumstances report with respect to the patient. It would be best practice to ensure that the MHO only receives the two mental health reports after as much prior discussion of the need for the application as is practicable. Where possible, such discussions should take place face-to-face. Exclusion of the MHO from the assessment process may adversely affect the quality of the assessment as well as that of the resulting proposed care plan. Early involvement of the MHO also gives time for the RMO and MHO to discuss and seek to resolve any differences of opinion prior to the application being made.

06 As a rule, the CTO application process should be characterised from beginning to end by co-operation and multi-disciplinary working between the medical practitioners providing the mental health reports, the MHO making the application and the other parties relevant to the application process, such as the patient's relatives and carers.

Which documents must be submitted as part of the application? What must the application contain? (section 63)

07 An application for a CTO consists of:

- two mental health reports prepared by the medical practitioners under section 57 of the Act and examined in paragraphs 9 to 37 of this chapter;
- the mental health officer's report prepared under section 61 of the Act and examined in paragraphs 38 - 63 of this chapter; and
- the proposed care plan produced by the MHO under section 62 of the Act and examined in paragraphs 64 - 73 of this chapter.

08 The application must also specify the matters listed at section 63(2)(a) of the Act, namely:

- the compulsory measures that are being sought in relation to the patient (i.e. which of the compulsory measures listed at section 66(1) of the Act are being sought);
- the medical treatment, community care services, relevant services and any other forms of treatment, care or service which it is proposed will be provided to the patient; and
- the name of the hospital whose managers will appoint the patient's RMO. (This is only required where the proposed CTO seeks to impose community-based requirements.)

chapter three

Preparing a Mental Health Report (Section 57-58)

09 Paragraphs 10 to 33 of this chapter describe what is required of a medical practitioner when preparing a mental health report as part of a CTO application.

Who can carry out the medical examination which precedes the preparation of the mental health report?

10 Section 58 of the Act provides that the two medical examinations can be carried out by either:
- two approved medical practitioners; or
- one approved medical practitioner and the patient's general practitioner.

11 Where the patient already has an RMO, it would be expected that that RMO would carry out one of the examinations. With respect to the second examination, it would be best practice for this to be carried out, wherever possible, by the patient's general practitioner as he/she can draw on knowledge and experience of the patient and their family, and often bring the benefit of an established, pre-existing relationship with the patient. The general practitioner can therefore provide an assessment of the patient's mental state which incorporates other dimensions of the patient's medical history which may not be available to an approved medical practitioner, including physical illnesses and treatments, and can offer a valuable insight into how these may interact with whatever mental health difficulties are at issue. The general practitioner is also best placed to express the potential contribution of primary care services to care and treatment plans in anticipation of playing an important longer term role in contributing to the patient's rehabilitation and recovery.

12 When it is not possible or practicable for the patient's general practitioner to carry out one of the medical examinations, an approved medical practitioner will undertake the examination. In such an event, the approved medical practitioner must not work directly with the other practitioner to ensure the independence of the opinion given. Wherever possible, however, it is important that the second examination be carried out by a practitioner who has previous knowledge of the patient. For details on the avoidance of conflicts of interest with respect to the medical examinations, see paragraphs 14 to 16 of this chapter.

13 Any practitioner who provides a mental health report may be required by the Tribunal to attend any subsequent hearing. The Tribunal's Rules of Procedure outlines the procedures relating to a citation to attend to payments which may be made to any person attending a Tribunal hearing.

Conflicts of interest in relation to the medical examination

14 **The Mental Health (Conflict of Interest) (Scotland) (No 2) Regulations 2005** specifies the circumstances where there is or there is not to be considered a conflict of interest in rclation to compulsory treatment orders. Considered a conflict when:

- either medical practitioner is related to the patient in any degree specified (see list of prohibited degrees of relationship below);
- the two medical practitioners are related to each other in any degree specify (see list of prohibited degrees of relationship below);
- where the CTO proposes the detention in an independent health care service and either medical practitioner is employed by or contracted to provide services in or to that health care service;
- where the CTO authorises detention in an NHS hospital and both medical practitioners are employed or contracted to provide services in or to that hospital;
- prohibited degrees of relationship are – child, grandchild, parent, grandparent, wife, husband, sister, brother, daughter-in-law, son-in-law, mother-in-law, father-in-law, sister-in-law, brother-in-law, cohabitee and any child, grandchild, parent, grandparent, sister or brother of a cohabitee.

15 An examination is permitted to be carried out even where there is a conflict of interest if:

- the conflict of interest is in terms of regulations 4(1)(c) or (d) (see third and fourth bullet points of paragraph 14 above);
- failure to carry out a medical examination would result in delay which would involve serious risk to the health, safety and welfare of the patient or to the safety of other persons; and
- if one of the medical practitioners is a consultant and the other practitioners does not work directly with or under the supervision of that consultant.

16 Although the Act makes no reference to conflicts of interest which may arise in relation to the MHO's involvement in the detention process, an

MHO should nonetheless bear in mind that it would be best practice to avoid becoming involved in the detention of a colleague, relative or friend. An MHO who believes that a conflict of interest might arise should request local authority employers to designate another MHO to deal with the case. Where no other MHO can be designated, the MHO should declare this possible conflict of interest in the MHO's report prepared under section 61 of the Act.

When must the two medical examinations be carried out? Should the examinations be carried out separately?

17 Section 58 of the Act states that the two medical examinations should be carried out separately. In such circumstances, the second medical examination must be completed no later than 5 days after the first (that is, 5 calendar days, not working days).

18 However, if the patient gives consent, the examinations may take place at the same time. If the patient is incapable of granting consent, then the examinations may take place at the same time if the patient's named person, guardian or welfare attorney (i.e. a welfare guardian or welfare attorney holding the relevant powers under the Adults with Incapacity (Scotland) Act 2000) has granted his/her consent. It would be best practice for the medical practitioners to advise the patient of his/her right to separate examinations. It would also be best practice to ensure that where the examinations are carried out at the same time, they record in the mental health reports their reasons for not carrying out the examinations separately.

What form of medical examination should be carried out?

19 Medical practitioners should ensure that they not only examine the current medical state of the patient, they should also weigh up that current medical state with the practitioner's experience of the past episodes of the patient's illness and crucially, previous adherence to treatment. Medical examinations as part of an application for long-term compulsion should be based not only on a 'moment-in-time' mental state examination but also on a consideration of the patient's past psychiatric history and a prediction of the success of longer-term care and treatment. In the course of these considerations, practitioners would be expected to seek input from the patient's MHO to inform their assessment of the patient's condition. Similarly, the views of other

relevant parties who currently provide or are likely to provide care and treatment to the patient in the future should be sought while all the time respecting issues of patient confidentiality.

20 Medical practitioners should always ensure that the examination takes place at a time and place which is convenient and safe for the patient as well as the practitioners. They should be sensitive to the wishes of the patient to have their independent advocate, named person, etc present at the medical examination. It would be good practice for the practitioners to discuss with the patient whom they would wish to be present at any interviews which are for assessment purposes. While the patient's choice should be accepted to the greatest extent possible, it will be a matter of judgement for the practitioner to establish a balance between the patient's need for support and the circumstances in which a full assessment can take place. In that context, given that the independent advocate's role includes helping the patient articulate his/her views, that advocate may be extremely helpful in both supporting the patient and helping the practitioners achieve a greater understanding of the patient's perspective which will in turn assist in their assessment. This may also be the case with a relative, carer or named person.

21 In all cases where the patient is being examined, sensitivity should be shown to ensure that the patient is supported but not overwhelmed by too many people in the room where the examination is taking place. It will be important to try to ensure that the patient does not feel as if he/she is on trial where an assessment in being made.

22 Where a patient is in the community (and therefore not subject to compulsory measures) when the medical examination takes place but refuses to consent to the examination, the medical practitioners and the MHO will need to decide whether they have each been able to carry out a good enough assessment. If they cannot, and if sufficient concern exists about the patient's need for treatment and the potential risk to the patient or others, then consideration should be given to whether the patient meets the criteria for the granting of a short-term detention certificate. This would allow for a period of hospital detention during which a fuller and more satisfactory examination of the patient can take place. *(For further information on the process of granting a short-term detention certificate, see Part 6 of the Act or Chapter 2 of this Volume of the Code of Practice.)*

chapter three

What are the criteria for long-term compulsion which must be met and which must be referred to in the mental health report?

23 Before an application for a CTO is made, certain requirements need to be met. These are set down in section 57(2) to (5) of the Act. One of these is that each of the medical practitioners who examines the patient must be satisfied that the criteria listed at section 57(3) of the Act have been met. Quoting from section 57(3) of the Act, these criteria are:

> (a) that the patient has a mental disorder;
> (b) that medical treatment which would be likely to–
> (i) prevent the mental disorder worsening; or
> (ii) alleviate any of the symptoms, or effects, of the disorder;
> is available for the patient;
> (c) that if the patient were not provided with such medical treatment there would be a significant risk–
> (i) to the health, safety or welfare of the patient; or
> (ii) to the safety of any other person;
> (d) that because of the mental disorder the patient's ability to make decisions about the provision of such medical treatment is significantly impaired; and
> (e) that the making of a compulsory treatment order is necessary.

24 It is important to remember that the final criterion in the box above will be satisfied only if the patient will not accept treatment voluntarily and that treatment cannot be provided without recourse to compulsory measures.

What must the mental health report contain?

25 If the medical practitioner is satisfied that these criteria have been met, he/she must complete a 'mental health report'. It is recommended that pro forma CTO1, part 3 be used for this purpose. This report should refer to the points listed at section 57(4) of the Act. (There is no form prescribed in regulations for these treatments but a pro-forma, CTO1, may be found on the Scottish Executive's website at www.scotland.gov.uk/health/mentalhealthlaw.) Quoting from that section of the Act, the RMO must:

(a) state that the medical practitioner submitting the report is satisfied that the conditions mentioned in paragraphs (a) to (e) of subsection (3) above are met in respect of the patient;
(b) state, in relation to each of the conditions mentioned in paragraphs (b) to (e) of subsection (3) above, the medical practitioner's reasons for believing the condition to be met in respect of the patient;
(c) specify (by reference to the appropriate paragraph (or paragraphs) of the definition of "mental disorder" in section 328(1) of this Act) the type (or types) of mental disorder that the patient has;
(d) set out a description of–
  (i) the symptoms that the patient has of the mental disorder; and
  (ii) the ways in which the patient is affected by the mental disorder;
(e) specify the measures that should, in the medical practitioner's opinion, be authorised by the compulsory treatment order;
(f) specify the date or dates on which the medical practitioner carried out the medical examination mentioned in subsection (2) above; and
(g) set out any other information that the medical practitioner considers to be relevant.

26 As much information as possible regarding the points listed at section 57(4) (i.e. those quoted immediately above) should be included in the mental health report. Discussion of these points should cover, where appropriate and relevant:

- a description of the alternatives to compulsory powers which are considered to be unworkable or unlikely to succeed; and
- why the care and treatment options proposed and the compulsory measures recommended involve the minimum restriction on the freedom of the patient that is necessary in the circumstances.

27 The purpose of such discussions is to provide the patient's MHO with the widest scope possible within which to prepare the application. Similarly, it allows the Tribunal to make as informed a decision as possible with respect to the application. In this regard, it will be important for the medical practitioners to ensure that the mental health reports are drafted in language which is largely understandable to a non-medical reader.

chapter three

28 The MHO should not have to rely solely on the evidence provided in the mental health report when it comes to his/her knowledge of the patient's medical/mental state. The function of a mental health report provided by a medical practitioner is to reflect the communication between the medical practitioner and the MHO which has already taken place prior to the report being prepared, not serve as the communication between them.

What are the compulsory measures which a medical practitioner can recommend in a mental health report?

29 The measures which the medical practitioner may recommend in line with paragraph (e) of section 57(4) (quoted in the box above) are those listed at section 66(1) of the Act. Quoting from that sub-section of the Act, these are:

(a) the detention of the patient in the specified hospital;
(b) the giving to the patient, in accordance with Part 16 of this Act, of medical treatment;
(c) the imposition of a requirement on the patient to attend–
(i) on specified or directed dates; or
(ii) at specified or directed intervals;
specified or directed places with a view to receiving medical treatment;
(d) the imposition of a requirement on the patient to attend–
(i) on specified or directed dates; or
(ii) at specified or directed intervals;
specified or directed places with a view to receiving community care services, relevant services or any treatment, care or service;
(e) the imposition of a requirement on the patient to reside at a specified place;
(f) the imposition of a requirement on the patient to allow-
(i) the mental health officer;
(ii) the patient's responsible medical officer; or
(iii) any person responsible for providing medical treatment, community care services, relevant services or any treatment, care or service to the patient who is authorised for the purposes of this paragraph by the patient's responsible medical officer;
to visit the patient in the place where the patient resides;

(g) the imposition of a requirement on the patient to obtain the approval of the mental health officer to any proposed change of address; and

(h) the imposition of a requirement on the patient to inform the mental health officer of any change of address before the change takes effect.

30 It would be expected that a medical practitioner would only recommend imposing community-based compulsory powers in a limited range of circumstances. For example, a requirement to reside at a particular place should only be recommended in exceptional circumstances. Much will depend upon the individual circumstances of the patient who is subject to the application, but circumstances in which a medical practitioner might recommend recourse to community-based compulsory measures might include where:

- community-based powers would provide a safe and viable alternative to compulsory hospitalisation;
- a patient has previously relapsed whilst off medication in the community, and as a result, has presented a risk to themselves and/or others;
- all other means of trying to negotiate with the patient and maintain them in the community without compulsion have been tried and have failed; and
- alternatively, less restrictive approaches to secure and adequate adherence with necessary treatments have been shown to be impracticable.

31 Before recommending that community-based compulsory measures be applied for, the medical practitioner would be expected to demonstrate in the mental health report that issues such as those listed above, in addition to any others relevant to the patient's case, have been fully taken into consideration. In doing so, it will be important to demonstrate that consideration has been given to the potential impact of these community-based compulsory measures on any carers or other persons who live with and/or care for the patient.

chapter three

32 If it is expected that community-based compulsory measures would only be recommended under certain circumstances, as described above, consideration should similarly be given to whether community-based measures are being recommended as an alternative to hospital-based compulsory measures for the appropriate reasons. For example, community-based measures should not be recommended only because a hospital bed is not available or only because the carers or person(s) that the patient currently lives alongside do(es) not wish them to reside at that address. Best practice suggests that a medical practitioner would only recommend that the patient be treated in hospital where that patient requires the care, treatment and services which only a hospital in-patient service can provide.

33 The medical practitioner should, where relevant and practicable, seek input into the mental health report from appropriately qualified professionals, such as speech and language therapists, occupational therapists and clinical psychologists, where they would be able to contribute to the assessment process from their own areas of expertise. For example, it would be important for a medical practitioner to seek input from an appropriately qualified psychologist in relation to a complex assessment of impaired decision-making ability or a case involving a significant learning disability or personality disorder. Similarly, where psychological interventions are being recommended, input should be sought from the appropriately qualified party likely to be providing that intervention.

Further points to be covered in a mental health report: withholding notice

34 There are two further points which the approved medical practitioner must cover in the mental health reports in terms of section 57(5)(c). Note that these points are to be covered only by the approved medical practitioner, not by any non-approved medical practitioner who examines the patient. If two approved medical practitioners examine the patient, it would be best practice for the patient's RMO to deal with these two points. The points are:

- a statement as to whether or not written notice should be given to the patient of the fact that an application for a CTO is to be made; and
- a statement as to whether or not the practitioner considers the patient to be capable of arranging for a person to represent him/her at any future Tribunal hearing.

35 It would be best practice to only take decisions on these matters after engaging in as full prior consultation as possible with the patient's MHO and other members of the patient's multi-disciplinary team. The expectation is that notice of the application would always be given to the patient, and therefore, that it would only be withheld under exceptional circumstances. However, subject to any prior consultation with the patient's MHO and other relevant parties, it is acceptable to recommend withholding notice where such notice would be likely to cause significant harm to the patient or to another person (see section 57(6)). This could happen in a case where the patient is highly unsettled or likely to abscond and therefore become a risk to themselves through, for example, not taking medication.

36 The approved medical practitioner should be mindful of the fact that the MHO is under a duty to inform the patient of their rights in relation to the application later in the application process. Recommending that notice be withheld from the patient may cause the MHO serious difficulties in carrying out his/her duty to inform the patient of his/her rights with respect to the application under section 61. In such circumstances, it would be best practice for the RMO to discuss with the MHO the best and most sensitive way in which this duty can be carried out.

How similar must the two reports be to one another for the application process to proceed?

37 The CTO application cannot proceed if the two mental health reports do not come to similar conclusions about the patient's condition. For the application to proceed, the two reports must:

- agree on the category of primary mental disorder: that is, a report must specify at least one type of mental disorder that is also specified in the other report. (These types of mental disorder are defined in section 328(1) of the Act: i.e. mental illness; personality disorder; and learning disability.); and
- specify the same compulsory measures that should be authorised by the CTO. (These are the compulsory measures listed at section 66(1) of the Act.)

chapter three

Duties of the MHO once in receipt of two mental health reports

38 The MHO making the CTO application must comply with a range of duties before he/she submits the application to the Tribunal. These duties are set out in sections 59 to 63 of the Act and in paragraphs 38 to 73 of this Chapter of the Code of Practice. Paragraphs 40 to 57 of this chapter provide details of the duties which an MHO must carry out with respect to the patient. Paragraphs 58 to 73 then describe the process of completing a mental health officer's report and the proposed care plan.

39 Throughout the CTO application process, the MHO should have regard to the principles of the legislation and the other matters set out in sections 1 to 3 of the Act. In this context, it will be particularly important to have regard to the principles of ensuring that the patient can participate as fully as possible in the processes involved in applying for and determining the CTO and of providing such information and support to the patient as is necessary to facilitate that participation.

The MHO must identify the patient's named person

40 Section 59 of the Act states that the MHO must take all the steps that are practicable to ascertain the name and address of the patient's named person. The MHO should do this as soon as is practicable after the duty to make the application arises. Identifying the patient's named person may necessitate discussion with the RMO and/or other relevant professionals as to whether the patient has the capacity to nominate a named person.

41 It would be best practice for the MHO to first explain to the patient verbally and with a follow-up leaflet the status and rights of the named person as well as the role they can play in the CTO application process and beyond. The MHO will consequently also need to explain the difference between the roles of the named person and the independent advocate.

42 An MHO will need to be very familiar with the procedures outlined in Part 17 Chapter 1 of the Act regarding the nomination process of the named person. This is because under section 255 of the Act the MHO has a duty in certain circumstances and a power at other times to apply to the Tribunal for an order under section 257 to remove and replace an "apparent named person" (i.e. a person whom the MHO considers to be inappropriate to act in that role). The decision as to whether the apparent named person is inappropriate to act should not be made by the MHO alone but in consultation with other relevant members of the patient's multi-disciplinary team. The expectation is that the patient's right to choose whom he/she wishes to have as a named person would be respected. The MHO has no power to veto the patient's choice at the time of nomination, nor should they apply undue influence on the patient. The MHO should intervene using the powers given at section 255 only where there are clear and significant reasons for doing so. *(For further details regarding the nomination process of a named person, see Part 17 Chapter 1 of the Act or Chapter 6 Volume 1 of the Code of Practice.)*

43 The MHO should explain to the patient that in the absence of them nominating a named person, their primary carer shall (where they are aged 16 or over) become their named person. When ascertaining the identity of the named person and the primary carer, the MHO should be careful to respect the patient's rights with respect to confidentiality and to only disclose a minimal level of information about the patient's detention. The patient may after all wish a relative with whom they have a poor relationship to know little about their detention. The MHO should also explain the process whereby the patient can make a declaration under section 253 of the Act or an application under section 256 of the Act to prevent a particular individual being their named person.

44 As with all occasions where a named person is being nominated, the MHO should consider the impact on the nearest relative/primary carer where they are not nominated as the named person. This could be done through explaining to them the role of the named person and the rights of relatives/carers who are not the patient's named person.

chapter three

45 The MHO should also ascertain whether the named person is fully aware of the fact that they have been nominated as the named person and that they are in fact willing to take on that role. If they are, the MHO should explain to them what the role of named person entails; and the rights and responsibilities it confers on them (for example, with respect to making applications to the Tribunal).

46 It would also be best practice for the MHO to find out at this stage whether the patient has an advance statement and where it is located.

The MHO must notify certain parties that the application is being made

47 Section 60 of the Act states that before submitting the application to the Tribunal, the MHO must notify the following parties in writing that the application is being made. The parties are:

- the patient;
- the patient's named person; and
- the Commission.

48 The MHO must do this as soon as is practicable after the duty to prepare the application arises. Providing notice as early in the application process as possible enables the patient and the named person to take legal advice and prepare fully for the hearing.

49 Where the approved medical practitioner has recommended in his/her mental health report that notice of the application being made should be withheld from the patient, the MHO may override this recommendation. Section 60(2) of the Act states that the MHO may notify the patient of the application where he/she considers it appropriate to do so. Where the MHO does decide to override the approved medical practitioner's recommendation, he/she should have discussed in some detail with the medical practitioner the reasons for this decision. Moreover, in such cases, the MHO should record in writing his/her reasons for overriding the medical practitioner's original recommendation. This is particularly important in cases where the mental health report includes an assessment of high risk.

50 Although section 60 of the Act imposes a duty on the MHO to give notice to the patient (that is, give notice in writing), the MHO should always consider informing the patient and the named person orally in addition to the written notification. This will give the patient and the named person as much time as possible to prepare for the Tribunal hearing. Moreover, it would be best practice for an MHO, where practicable, to ensure that any written notification is hand-delivered (or sent by recorded delivery) to the patient so that the details, implications and importance of the notification and the application can be explained to the patient. There may be circumstances in which the MHO would want to seek the assistance of other members of the multi-disciplinary team to carry this out or to assist in carrying this out. It would also be best practice for the MHO to discuss with the patient whether they wish anyone else to be informed of the application, such as the primary carer, if they are not the named person, or their independent advocate, if the patient already has one.

The MHO must inform the patient of his/her rights

51 Section 61(2)(b) to (d) of the Act imposes on the MHO a range of further duties which must be carried out in advance of submitting the CTO application to the Tribunal. These include:

- a duty to inform the patient that the application is to be made;
- a duty to inform the patient of the availability of independent advocacy services; and
- a duty to take appropriate steps to ensure that the patient has the opportunity to make use of these advocacy services.

52 The MHO should not look at the process of complying with these duties as a simple 'tick-box exercise' as the manner of carrying out these duties will need to vary considerably from one patient to another. The onus is on the MHO to engage in a dynamic process which will allow him/her to demonstrate that the patient has been made aware of his/her rights in a manner which aims to ensure that he/she can gain the best possible understanding of these rights. The MHO may need to involve other members of the multi-disciplinary care team in this process, such as a clinical psychologist, ward nursing staff or CPN.

chapter three

53 Where the patient is hostile, indifferent or too ill to comprehend, the MHO should also consider making contact with the patient's relatives, carers, named person or independent advocate, as appropriate. The MHO should also always be willing to visit the patient more than once in an attempt to fulfil these duties. Merely putting a leaflet through the patient's letter-box without making further attempts to inform the patient of his/her rights would not be sufficient.

The MHO must interview the patient

54 Section 61(2)(a) of the Act imposes a duty on the MHO to interview the patient. The function of this interview is to permit the MHO to assess the impact of the suspected mental disorder on the individual's social functioning and to determine whether recourse to compulsory powers under the Act, as recommended in the mental health reports, is warranted. The interview could focus, on the one hand, on the points of contention between what the two medical practitioners have proposed in their mental health reports and, on the other, the views of the patient. Views on this subject should also be elicited from a range of sources beyond the interview with the patient, such as from any advance statement made by the patient; and, within the bounds of patient confidentiality, discussions with the patient's independent advocate, named person, carers, relatives or key worker.

55 As much prior notice of the interview as possible should be given to the patient to enable the patient's independent advocate, named person, etc to attend. However, the failure of any party to attend the interview should not be allowed to paralyse the application process. The interview should also be held in as private a space as possible and in a location that is as convenient and safe as possible for the patient as well as the MHO.

56 It is unlikely to ever be completely impracticable for an MHO to comply with the duty to interview the patient. Indeed, it may be necessary for an MHO to attempt on more than one occasion to interview the patient. Only in exceptional circumstances would an MHO not be able to comply with this duty: for example, where the patient is acutely psychotic and/or there is an immediate risk to the MHO's personal safety. In such circumstances, it would be best practice to meet the patient's named person, nearest relative, key worker, carers, etc instead. Where the MHO has been unable to comply with the interview requirement, he/she should

make a record of the actions taken, why these actions failed, and what alternatives were considered and followed up. By way of section 61(4)(d) of the Act, this record must be included in the mental health officer's report which accompanies the CTO application.

57 The following statements represent a non-exhaustive list of some best practice points which an MHO should comply with when carrying out these duties with respect to the patient. The MHO should:

- explain the CTO application process to the patient, including how the Tribunal hearing will operate, where it will take place, who will be in attendance etc…;
- advise the patient of his/her rights with respect to legal representation at the hearing. It would be good practice for an MHO to have knowledge of the solicitors in the local area willing to take on such work (although the MHO should be careful not to promote any one practice);
- inform the patient of the rights and responsibilities of the named person and then, if necessary and if this has not been done already, explain the process of nominating a named person;
- ask the key worker and/or RMO to impart any necessary information to the patient if the patient is hostile to interventions by the MHO;
- back up any information given to the patient orally with a leaflet setting out similar information so that the patient (and/or family members, carers, etc) can have the opportunity to assimilate the information at a later date. The MHO should ensure that a contact address/number is included in any such written information;
- contribute to making sure that any communication barriers are addressed by, for example, ensuring that a translator/interpreter is provided if necessary; ensuring that relevant documents are made available in Braille, audio-cassette format, etc…; and
- ascertain whether the patient wants or already has an independent advocate. This could include giving the patient oral and written information about local advocacy services as well as helping the patient make use of those services. One important task will be for the MHO to explain to the patient the difference between the functions of the named person, a legal advocate and an independent advocate.

chapter three

Preparing a mental health officer's report

58 Section 61(4) of the Act sets out the items that must be included in the MHO's report which accompanies the CTO application. These are:

- the name and address of the patient;
- the name and address of the patient's named person and the patient's primary carer, if they are known by the MHO;
- the steps which the MHO has taken to comply with the duties imposed on him/her by section 61(2) of the Act (these duties are described in paragraphs 38 to 46 above);
- the reason it was impracticable to interview the patient, if this proved to be the case;
- details of the personal circumstances of the patient in so far as they are relevant for the purposes of the application;
- the MHO's views on the 2 mental health reports relating to the patient;
- details of any advance statement which the patient has made (and not withdrawn), where known by the MHO; and
- any other information that the MHO considers relevant to the Tribunal's determination of the application.

59 In essence, the purpose of this report is to provide the Tribunal with:

- relevant background information relating to the patient;
- information on any previous periods of hospitalisation because of mental disorder (whether formal or informal) and their effect on the patient;
- confirmation that the patient has been made aware of his/her rights and the steps which the MHO has taken in this process;
- details of whether the patient has an advance statement and the extent to which the wishes set out in the advance statement have been taken into account in the proposals for the patient's care and treatment;
- the views of the MHO on the mental health reports and on the extent to which he/she supports the application, including the MHO's views on whether the criteria for compulsory powers are satisfied and on whether there are viable courses of action which could be taken other than those recommended in the mental health reports, particularly those which could avoid recourse to compulsory powers. To come to a view on these issues, the MHO may need on occasion to request a report from, for example, a clinical psychologist, an occupational therapist or a nurse therapist among others to complement the information provided by the medical practitioners in their mental health reports;

- an assessment of whether it is necessary to compel the patient to accept treatment and of how likely it is that the treatment could be provided informally. This is essential as the fundamental decision which the Tribunal hearing is making is whether the patient's autonomy should be overridden when it comes to making decisions about treatment. It is therefore crucial that the MHO address the appropriateness of each of the compulsory measures which the medical practitioners recommended in their mental health reports;
- the possible impact of the proposed compulsory measures on the patient's personal finances, particularly welfare benefits (for example, Income Support or Disability Living Allowance), housing costs, etc; and
- an indication as to the views of the patient's informal support networks, including the named person and carers. For example, if the MHO supports the medical recommendations and the CTO application but the carer does not, the report should contain information on the carer's suggested alternatives to compulsion and an account of why the MHO (and RMO etc) believe these alternatives are not viable.

60 It would be best practice for the MHO to include in the report the contact details of not just the named person and the primary carer, as is required by section 61(4)(b), but also the contact details of the wider care network, including the patient's advocate, where known, and any other relevant individuals who provide care and treatment.

61 An MHO is free to, and indeed expected to, express views on the mental health reports prepared by the medical practitioners, and in particular, views on the range of compulsory measures being recommended in the mental health reports. If the MHO disagrees with the reports, he/she should identify any deficiencies in the reports with regard to the explanation of whether the criteria for compulsory powers are met. However, there should be prior discussion with the medical practitioners in which these views or concerns are raised. The MHO should also consider whether the care and treatment proposed by the medical practitioners as well as the compulsory measures they recommended represent, in all the circumstances, the least restrictive environment in which the patient can be cared for and treated. This process will require the MHO to have a knowledge of the availability of alternative supports and services as well as an assessment of whether these would be appropriate and viable in the circumstances.

chapter three

62 Where the practitioners have recommended community-based compulsory measures in the mental health reports, it would be good practice for the MHO to consider the extent to which the issues described at paragraphs 29 to 33 above have been taken into account before including these compulsory measures in the final CTO application.

63 While it may be that the MHO legitimately reaches the conclusion that, in his/her view, the criteria for compulsory measures are not in fact satisfied, the assessment should include an analysis of the likely impact on the patient's health, safety and welfare if the care and treatment does not proceed on a compulsory basis. The decision to formally dissent from the opinions offered in mental health reports should only be taken following detailed discussion with the medical practitioners, wherever this is practicable. Where such legitimate professional differences still exist, it is for the Tribunal to make a judgement on whether or not to grant the application.

chapter three

Preparing a "proposed care plan"

64 In terms of section 62(2) of the Act, the MHO must prepare a "proposed care plan" as part of the application for a CTO. Section 62(3) to (8) of the Act sets out the content of the proposed care plan. In essence, the proposed care plan revolves around four factors:

- the patient's needs;
- the actions proposed to meet those needs;
- the objectives of those actions; and
- the parties who are carrying out those actions.

65 Information on these four factors is then broken down into three further categories. These are:

- the patient's needs, etc with respect to medical treatment for mental disorder;
- the patient's needs, etc with respect to community care or other relevant services;
- the patient's needs, etc with respect to other forms of care and treatment.

66 It is imperative to remember in the preparation of the proposed care plan that the Act provides a precise definition of what constitutes medical treatment: that is, medical treatment under the Act means *medical treatment for the patient's mental disorder*. Section 329 of the Act states that within this definition of medical treatment is included: nursing; care; psychological intervention; habilitation and rehabilitation (including education and training in work, social and independent living skills).

67 The proposed care plan should also make clear which elements of the care package are being provided with the patient's agreement and which it is proposed will be provided on a compulsory basis. However, in order to maintain a holistic approach to the patient's care and treatment, it is important that compulsory and non-compulsory elements are expressed in a way which underlines that the efficacy of the overall plan depends on the delivery of all the elements as a unified whole, wherever this is the case. Moreover, the proposed care plan should spell out which of *each* of the compulsory and non-compulsory powers are essential to the overall efficacy of the plan. This then helps the Tribunal decide what might be specified in the CTO as a recorded matter. *(For further information on "recorded matters", see section 64(4)(a)(ii) of the Act.)*

chapter three

68 The information with respect to needs, actions, objectives and parties carrying out those actions should be set out in the table on pro forma CTO1, part 4 which is recommended to be used for this purpose. The MHO will also have to explain reasons for coming to the conclusions laid out in that table. (There is no form prescribed in regulations for these treatments but a pro-forma, CTO1, may be found on the Scottish Executive's website at www.scotland.gov.uk/health/mentalhealthlaw.) The questions to which the MHO will be expected to respond include:

- how do the elements of the proposed care plan above comply with the principles of the Act and other matters at sections 1 to 3 of the Act (e.g. the principle of least restrictive alternative)?
- what alternatives were considered to the options proposed? Why were these alternatives deemed to be not workable or practicable?
- what contingency plans are in place if the options proposed do not work, including crisis management contingency plans?
- to what extent does this care plan reflect the wishes of the patient as expressed in any advance statement or elsewhere? If any of these wishes have not been respected, why not?
- who was consulted in the process of drawing up this proposed care plan? To what extent are the views of those consulted reflected in the plan?
- how have issues of risk (either to the patient or others) been taken into consideration in the drawing up of the plan? What form of risk assessment has been carried out?

69 The proposed care plan should also describe the patient's un-met needs, where these exist, and why these needs are not being met or cannot be met. Providing this information affords the Tribunal a fuller view of the patient's case and of the care package.

70 The MHO should prepare the proposed care plan in close consultation with the practitioners who produced the mental health reports and with all other persons/agencies who will be providing services, treatment or care to the patient. All these parties would be expected to contribute willingly and fully to its preparation. In effect, the MHO should be producing a plan proposed by the whole multi-disciplinary team. As such, the burden of its preparation should not be shouldered by the MHO alone. It will also be important for the MHO to recognise the potentially vital contributions which the patient (as well as the patient's relatives, carers, independent advocate, as appropriate) can make to the process of preparing the proposed care plan.

chapter three

71 Occasions may arise where the MHO disagrees with key elements of what is being proposed both in the mental health reports and the proposed care plan. The MHO should, however, highlight such differences of opinion and propose alternative courses of action where these are thought to be available, viable and appropriate. It would then be for the Tribunal to grant or refuse the application in light of all the information presented to it.

72 The process of developing a proposed care plan will be informed by local procedures and protocols relating to assessment and care management and/or the Care Programme Approach. The crucial difference is that the preparation of a proposed care plan is a specialist task for the purposes of the CTO application. Well developed systems for assessment and care management, care programming and Single Shared Assessment should greatly enhance and facilitate the development of a proposed care plan.

73 It would be expected that where a proposed care plan is proposing, for example, a psychological intervention, a psychologist or other appropriately qualified person making that intervention would have been consulted and involved in the assessment process. Such involvement may be particularly important where the patient's diagnosis of primary mental disorder is learning disability or personality disorder or where the plan includes psychological interventions which are intended to be implemented without the patient's consent such as behaviour modification programmes.

chapter three

Submitting the application to the Tribunal and the Tribunal's determination of the application

74 For information on the process of submitting the application to the Tribunal, see the Tribunal's Rules of Procedure.

75 The flowchart on page 88 explains the options which are open to the Tribunal when determining a CTO application as well as the statutory duties which must be complied with subsequent to a CTO being made.

76 Once the application has been submitted to the Tribunal, the patient's RMO should give the patient a copy of the application papers and, more importantly, be available to discuss the application, explain the process and answer any questions which the patient may have. This applies whether the patient is in hospital or in the community at the time of the application. It would also be expected that the RMO ensures that the patient's independent advocate is informed of the time and date of the hearing so that he/she can support the patient throughout the Tribunal process.

When must the Tribunal determine the application? (sections 68 and 69)

77 Where a patient is subject to a short-term detention certificate or an extension certificate, that patient may be detained in hospital and treated under Part 16 of the Act under the authority of section 68 of the Act for a further 5 working days once the CTO application has been submitted. This 5 working day extension period begins at the point when the short-term detention certificate or the extension certificate expires. Note that it does not begin when the application is submitted to the Tribunal.

78 For example, if an application is submitted to the Tribunal in respect of a patient on day 13 of the short-term detention certificate, the time period within which the Tribunal must determine the application is the 15 days of the short-term detention certificate which are left to run plus the 5 working days added by way of section 68(2)(a) of the Act. If the application is submitted on day 2 of the extension certificate, the time period within which the application must be determined is the 1 remaining working day of the extension certificate plus the additional 5 working days added by section 68(2)(a). In terms of section 69 of the Act, the Tribunal is required to determine before the expiry of that period of 5 working days whether or not to make an interim CTO. *(For further information on an interim CTO, see section 65 of the Act and Chapter 4 of this Volume of the*

Code of Practice.) If the Tribunal does not make an interim CTO, then it is obliged to determine the application for the CTO within that period of 5 working days.

Who must be allowed to give evidence to the Tribunal? (section 64(2) and (3))

79 In terms of section 64(2) of the Act, a wide range of parties must be allowed to make either oral or written representation and to lead or produce evidence to the Tribunal. These parties are:

- the patient;
- the patient's named person;
- any guardian of the patient;
- any welfare attorney of the patient who has the relevant powers;
- the patient's mental health officer;
- the medical practitioners who submitted the mental health reports which accompany the application;
- if the patient has a responsible medical officer, that officer;
- the patient's primary carer;
- any curator *ad litem* appointed in respect of the patient by the Tribunal; and
- any other person appearing to the Tribunal to have an interest in the application (for example, the patient's nearest relative if they are not the primary carer; the patient's or the medical practitioner's lawyer; other medical practitioner or clinical psychologist called to give evidence; key worker or named nurse; the Commission, etc).

Can someone be compelled to attend a Tribunal hearing?

80 Yes. Any person can be compelled to attend a Tribunal hearing (see Schedule 2, Part 3, paragraph 12). Similarly, the Tribunal has the power to require any person to produce evidence for any hearing. Sanctions can be imposed for non-compliance, without reasonable excuse, with a request to attend or produce evidence for any hearing. Further details on this issue can be found in the Tribunal's Rules of Procedure. The Tribunal also has the power to pay allowances and expenses to persons attending a Tribunal hearing.

81 A Tribunal hearing could still go ahead in the absence of any individual. It is up to the individual Tribunal panel, however, to decide whether to proceed with or postpone the hearing in the event of one or more of the attendees not turning up.

chapter three

Which criteria does the Tribunal use in determining whether to make a CTO?

82 The criteria which the Tribunal uses in determining whether or not to make a CTO are set out in section 64(5) of the Act. Quoting from that sub-section of the Act, these are:

> (a) that the patient has a mental disorder;
> (b) that medical treatment which would be likely to–
> (i) prevent the mental disorder worsening; or
> (ii) alleviate any of the symptoms, or effects, of the disorder;
> is available for the patient;
> (c) that if the patient were not provided with such medical treatment there would be a significant risk–
> (i) to the health, safety or welfare of the patient; or
> (ii) to the safety of any other person;
> (d) that because of the mental disorder the patient's ability to make decisions about the provision of such medical treatment is significantly impaired;
> (e) that the making of a compulsory treatment order in respect of the patient is necessary; and
> (f) where the Tribunal does not consider it necessary for the patient to be detained in hospital, such other conditions as may be specified in regulations.

83 The above criteria are cumulative: that is, all of them must be met before the order can be made.

84 With respect to criterion (f) in the list above, there are currently no plans to exercise this regulation-making power. This situation will, however, be kept under review.

chapter three

CONSIDERATION OF A COMPULSORY TREATMENT ORDER APPLICATION – FLOWCHART

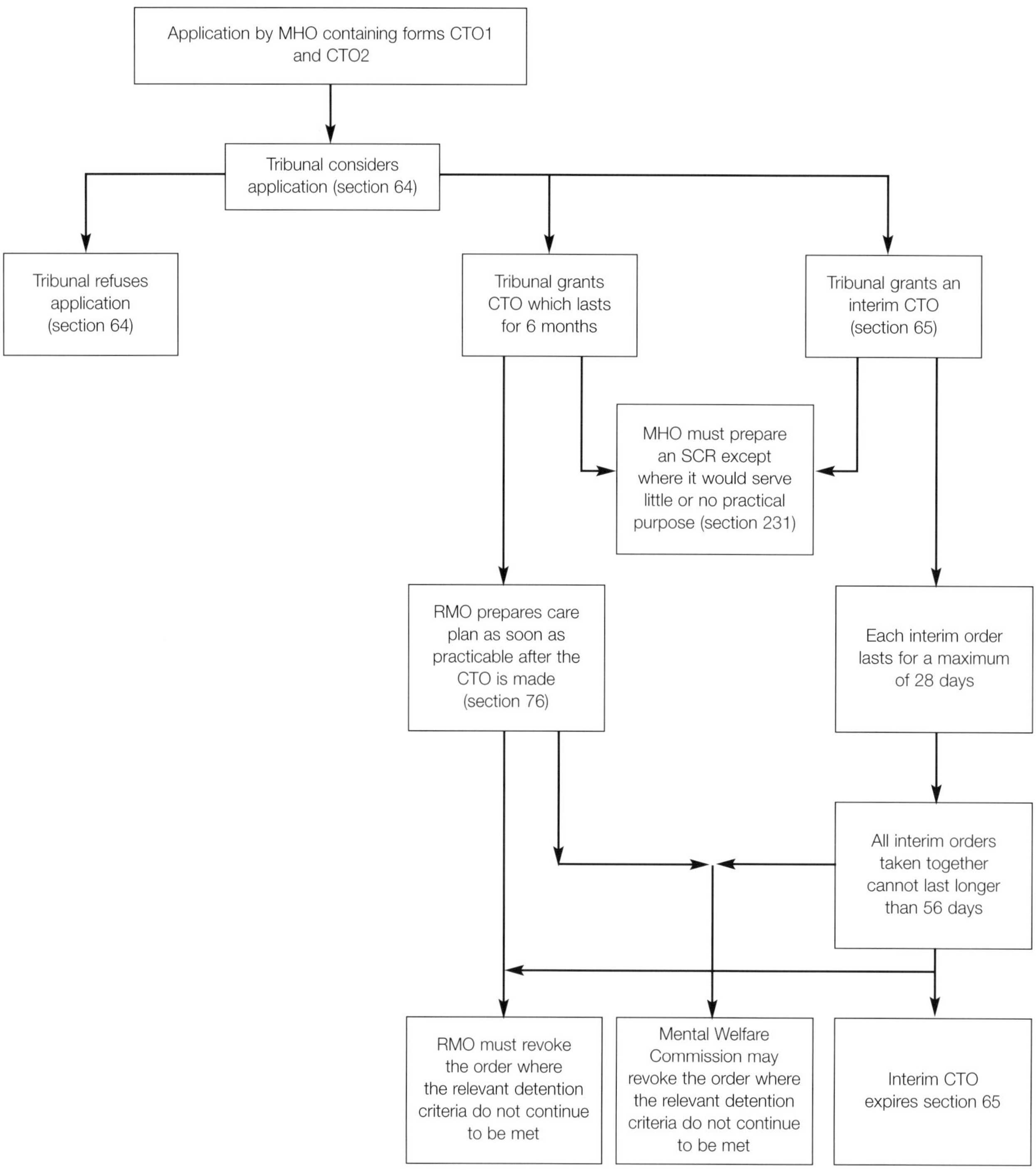

chapter three

What can the Tribunal authorise with respect to the CTO application?

85 The Tribunal has three options. It can refuse the application (this outcome is dealt with in paragraph 86 of this chapter); it can grant the CTO (see paragraphs 87 to 93); or it can grant an interim compulsory treatment order (see paragraphs 94 to 97).

The Tribunal can refuse the application (section 64(4)(b))

86 Where the Tribunal is satisfied that the relevant detention criteria are not met in respect of the patient, it must refuse to grant the application. In such cases, it would be expected that, where the patient was subject to a short-term detention certificate or an extension certificate immediately before the hearing, the RMO would revoke that detention certificate. If the patient is ultimately to be discharged from hospital as a result of the application being refused, it would be best practice for the RMO, in consultation with the other members of the patient's multi-disciplinary team, to oversee the drawing up and implementing of a discharge plan of care. This will enable the RMO and the multi-disciplinary team to comply with the duty placed on them by way of section 1(6) of the Act to have regard to the importance of the provision of appropriate services to the person who is, or has been, subject to compulsory powers.

The Tribunal can grant the application for a CTO (section 64(4)(a))

87 If all the conditions set out in section 64(5) of the Act are met, then the Tribunal may make an order containing the elements outlined at sections 64(4)(a), 64(6) to (8) and 66(1) of the Act. These elements are described in the following paragraphs. In summary, they are:

- a series of compulsory measures;
- recorded matters;
- the type of mental disorder which the patient has; and
- the name of the hospital the managers of which are responsible for appointing the patient's RMO (where community-based measures have been authorised).

88 An order will authorise a series of compulsory measures for a period of 6 months beginning with the day on which the CTO is made. This will be a combination of the compulsory measures listed at section 66(1) of the Act. Note that if the order authorises community-based compulsory measures, it must include a record of the name of the hospital whose managers will be responsible for appointing an approved medical practitioner to act as the patient's RMO. The compulsory measures which can be granted are:

- the detention of the patient in hospital;
- the giving of medical treatment to the patient in accordance with Part 16 of the Act;
- imposing on the patient a requirement to attend certain places at certain times for the purpose of receiving medical treatment (this is sometimes called "an attendance requirement");
- imposing on the patient a requirement to attend certain places at certain times for the purpose of receiving community care services, or other relevant services or treatment (this is similarly sometimes called "an attendance requirement");
- imposing on the patient a requirement to reside at a specified place (this is sometimes called "a residency requirement");
- imposing on the patient a requirement to allow certain parties to visit the patient in the place where he/she lives (these parties could be, for example, the patient's MHO or RMO);
- imposing on the patient a requirement to obtain the approval of his/her MHO to any proposed change of address; and
- imposing on the patient a requirement to inform his/her MHO of any change of address before that change of address takes effect.

89 The Act states at section 66(1)(c) and (d) that an attendance requirement may require a patient to attend "on specified or directed dates; or at specified or directed intervals" for medical treatment, community care services or other services. Section 66(3) defines "directed" as meaning "in accordance with directions given by the patient's RMO" and "specified" as meaning "specified in the compulsory treatment order". Where the Tribunal grants a compulsory treatment order which includes an attendance requirement, it has therefore two options. The first option is to specify in that order the times or dates on which the patient must attend for treatment. This could mean that the order would explicitly state that the patient must attend for treatment, for example, every second Tuesday or twice a week. The second option is to allow such

chapter three

detail to be left to the discretion of the patient's RMO. It is important to bear in mind that where the first option is chosen, an application would have to be made to the Tribunal under section 95 of the Act to vary the compulsory treatment order if the patient's RMO wishes to vary the times or dates on which the patient must attend for treatment. However, no such application would have to be made if the dates on which or the intervals at which the patient must attend for treatment are not specified in the order but are instead left to directions to be given by the RMO.

90 It should be noted that where the Tribunal authorises a "residency requirement" by way of section 66(1)(e), the address at which the patient must reside is specified in the order. This means therefore that if the RMO wishes a different address to be specified, he/she must make an application to the Tribunal under section 95 of the Act for an order which would vary the address specified in the compulsory treatment order.

91 In addition to the compulsory measures listed at section 66(1) of the Act, an order can specify "recorded matters". These are the particular types of medical treatment, community care services, relevant services or any other form of treatment, care or service which the Tribunal wishes to mark out as being essential to the care package. The Tribunal may wish to make something a recorded matter because where a recorded matter is not being provided to a patient over the course of the CTO, the patient's RMO is under a duty to bring this fact to the attention of the Tribunal in terms of section 96(3) of the Act. The Commission has the power to do likewise in terms of section 98 of the Act. On being informed of a failure to provide a recorded matter, the Tribunal will decide whether it wishes to vary the measures or recorded matters specified in the CTO or else revoke the CTO entirely. *For more information on the procedures for varying and/or revoking a CTO, see Part 7 Chapter 4 of the Act or Chapter 5 of this Volume of the Code of Practice.*

92 A CTO must also record the type(s) of mental disorder which the patient has. These types are listed in the Act at section 328(1): i.e. mental illness, personality disorder, or learning disability.

chapter three

93 As a result of the various representations made to the Tribunal, it may decide to specify in the order different, additional or fewer compulsory measures from those included in the application in terms of section 64(6) of the Act. It should be noted once again that these compulsory measures are those listed at section 66(1) of the Act. However, the Tribunal may only specify different compulsory measures in the order where it has complied with the two following requirements:

- it must give notice to all the parties listed at section 64(3) of the Act (see paragraph 79 of this Chapter above for further details) setting out that it is proposing to specify compulsory measures other than or additional to those contained in the CTO application. It must also set out what those compulsory measures are. However, the Tribunal need not provide written notification if the affected parties are present at the Tribunal hearing; and
- it must allow these parties the chance to make representation to the Tribunal in relation to what is proposed or to lead or produce evidence.

The Tribunal can authorise an interim compulsory treatment order (section 65)

94 The Tribunal may decide that it does not wish to grant a full 6 month CTO. It may instead grant a shorter order: an interim CTO. This outcome could happen where, for example, the Tribunal does not feel it has enough information on which to base their decision about the full CTO; where it wishes to seek further evidence from another party such as a medical practitioner, psychologist, social care provider, carer or relative; or where the patient and his/her representatives require further time in which to prepare their evidence. An interim CTO may also be granted where any person who has an interest in the proceedings makes an application for one.

95 The criteria which must be met before an interim CTO can be made are very similar to the criteria to those for a CTO. As set out in section 65(6) of the Act, they are:

- that the patient has a mental disorder;
- that medical treatment which would be likely to prevent the mental disorder worsening or to alleviate any of the symptoms, or effects, of the disorder, is available for the patient;

- that if the patient were not provided with such medical treatment there would be a significant risk to the health, safety or welfare of the patient, or to the safety of any other person;
- that because of mental disorder the patient's ability to make decisions about the provision of such medical treatment is significantly impaired; and
- that it is necessary to make an interim compulsory treatment order (i.e. that the treatment cannot be provided without recourse to compulsory measures).

96 An interim CTO may last for any period of up to 28 days. The Tribunal may grant more than one interim CTO in respect of a patient. However, the total period for all the interim CTOs granted taken together may not exceed a period of 56 consecutive days.

97 An interim CTO can authorise the same compulsory measures as those authorised by a 'full' compulsory treatment order. These are the measures listed at section 66(1) of the Act (see paragraph 88 above). Like a CTO, an interim CTO must also include details of the hospital whose managers are responsible for appointing the patient's RMO if it specifies community-based requirements.

98 Before an interim CTO can be made, the parties referred to at section 65(5) must be given the opportunity to make representation to the Tribunal and to lead/produce evidence.

Interaction of CTO or interim CTO with other orders and certificates

99 Section 70 of the Act states that where a patient is detained in hospital on the authority of a short-term detention certificate, and where a CTO or an interim CTO is made in respect of him/her, then the short-term detention certificate is revoked on the making of the CTO or interim CTO.

100 Section 75 states that where a patient who is subject to an interim CTO and where a CTO is made in respect of that patient, then the interim CTO is revoked.

chapter three

Statutory duties with respect to an application for a Compulsory Treatment Order

Which party must provide information or notification?	Timescale	Whom must they give this information or notification to?	What specific information must they provide?
Medical practitioner providing a mental health report (sections 57 and 58)	No timescale is specified in the Act. Note, however, that the Code of Practice makes clear that the report should be transmitted to the MHO as quickly as is practicable as the MHO has only 14 days in which to make the application. The clock starts running on this 14 day period when the second of the 2 medical examinations has taken place.	Mental Health Officer	The mental health report must: • state that the medical practitioner is satisfied that the conditions of 57(3)(a) to (e) are met; • state, for each of the conditions of 57(3)(b) to (e), the medical practitioner's reasons for believing that condition to be met; • specify the type (or types) of mental disorder that the patient has; • describe the symptoms of the mental disorder that the patient has and the ways in which the patient is affected by the mental disorder; • specify the compulsory measures that should, in his/her opinion, be authorised by the CTO; • specify the date or dates on which the medical practitioner carried out the medical examination; and • set out any other information that the medical practitioner considers to be relevant.
MHO (sections 57 & 63)	Within 14 days beginning with the later, or latest, of the medical examinations	They must prepare the CTO application and submit it to the Tribunal	1. With respect to the mental health reports, the MHO should ensure that: • at least one type of mental disorder is specified in both reports; • they specify the same compulsory measures that should be authorised by the CTO; • the mental health report prepared by an AMP states a view as to; • whether notice of the application should be given to the patient under s.60(1); • whether the patient is capable of arranging for a person to represent them in connection with the application. 2. The MHO must submit to the Tribunal: • the mental health officer's report; • the proposed care plan; • the 2 mental health reports; and • the CTO application.

Statutory duties with respect to an application for a Compulsory Treatment Order – continued

Which party must provide information or notification?	Timescale	Whom must they give this information or notification to?	What specific information must they provide?
MHO (section 59; Part 17, Chapter 1)	As soon as practicable after the duty to make the application arises	The Tribunal or the Commission, where applicable.	The MHO must take such steps as are reasonably practicable to ascertain the name and address of the patient's named person. He/she should comply with the provisions of Part 17 Chapter 1 of the Act with respect to the nomination of a named person.
MHO (section 60)	As soon as practicable after the duty to make the application arises	• the patient; • the named person; • the Commission.	The MHO must give notice to those parties that the application is to be made. If the view set out in one of the mental health reports (that is, the report by an AMP) is that notice should not be given to the patient, the MHO need not give that notice. However, if the MHO considers it appropriate to give that notice anyway, the MHO may do so.
MHO (section 61)	Before the application is made	The patient	The MHO must carry out a range of duties with respect to the patient: • he/she must interview the patient. If this is impracticable, then the MHO need not do so; • he/she must inform the patient that an application is to be made (if not previously notified under section 60(1)(a) of the Act); • he/she must inform the patient of his/her rights in relation to the application; • he/she must inform him/her of the availability of independent advocacy services and take appropriate steps to ensure that the patient has the opportunity of making use of those services.

chapter three

Statutory duties with respect to an application for a Compulsory Treatment Order

Which party must provide information or notification?	Timescale	Whom must they give this information or notification to?	What specific information must they provide?
MHO (section 61)	As part of the CTO application	To be submitted to the Tribunal	The MHO must prepare a report under section 61(4) stating: • the name and address of the patient; • if known by the MHO, the name and address of the patient's named person and the patient's primary carer; • the steps taken by the MHO to interview the patient, and, if it was impracticable to interview the patient, the reason why; • details of the patient's personal circumstances in so far as they are relevant to the application; • the MHO's views on the mental health reports; • details of any advance statement made by the patient (and not withdrawn), if known; and • any other information the MHO considers relevant
MHO (section 62)	As part of the CTO application	To be submitted to the Tribunal	The MHO must prepare a proposed care plan stating: • the type of mental disorder which the patient has; • the patient's needs (in terms of section 62(5)(b)&(c); • the medical treatment and services it is proposed to provide to the patient (in terms of section 62(5)(d), (e) & (f); • the objectives of the medical treatment and the services it is proposed to provide for the patient (in terms of section 62(5)(l); • which of the 8 compulsory measures listed at section 66(1) it is proposed that the CTO should authorise; • the name and address of the hospital in which the patient is to be detained or of the hospital whose managers are responsible for appointing the patient's RMO if the patient is to be subject to community-based measures; and • which of the forms of medical treatment and other services it is proposed to provide on a compulsory basis (in terms of section 62(5)(j).

chapter 4

the compulsory treatment order and the interim compulsory treatment order in operation (part 7 chapters 2, 3 & 7 or sections 72 to 76 and 127 to 129)

chapter four

Introduction

This chapter outlines the processes which should be followed immediately as a consequence of a CTO or an interim CTO being made. These include, for example, the process by which an interim CTO is revoked; an RMO's duty to prepare a care plan; and the processes by which compulsory measures are suspended. It does not deal with the processes associated with formal reviews of the CTO which are examined in chapter 5 of the Code of Practice. It also does not consider the process of transferring patients subject to a CTO or an interim CTO from one hospital to another. That issue is dealt with in Chapter 14 of Volume 1. Transfers between hospitals in Scotland are dealt with in Chapter 9 of Volume 2, while Chapter 14 of Volume 1 deals with transfers into or out of Scotland.

Transferring the patient to hospital once a CTO or interim CTO has been made (section 67)

01 Section 67 of the Act relates to a patient subject to a CTO or to an interim CTO which either authorises the patient's detention in a specified hospital or imposes on the patient a requirement to reside at a specified place. If the patient needs to be transferred to the hospital or other place specified in the CTO or interim CTO, authority to do so is provided by way of section 67. This transfer under the authority of section 67 must take place within 7 days of the CTO or interim CTO being made.

02 Section 67 only authorises the patient's transfer to a hospital or other place specified in the order. It does not in itself provide an authority to detain the patient during this period. Any authority to detain the patient during this period would come from the CTO or ICTO. In any rare occasion where the patient is to be found on premises to which it is not possible to obtain entry before this transfer takes place, it may be necessary to seek a warrant under Part 19 of the Act which would authorise, for example, a police constable to enter those premises. *(For further information on such warrants, see Chapter 15 of Volume 1 of the Code of Practice.)*

03 Where it is thought likely that the patient will have to be removed from one place to another after the CTO is made, a contingency plan for this transfer should have been drawn up and, where practicable, presented to the Tribunal before the order is made in order to provide it with as full a view of the patient's situation as possible. Such a contingency plan, although not part of the CTO application, could be appended to the proposed care plan forming part of the CTO application.

04 It is best practice to ensure that all parties have agreed their respective roles and responsibilities in this contingency plan in advance of the transfer taking place. It would be expected that such agreement would be in line with the roles and responsibilities allocated to each group within the relevant, locally developed psychiatric emergency plan.

05 It is important to note that no formal application is required for this power. The power has effect automatically once the CTO or interim CTO is made.

Operation of an interim CTO (Part 7, Chapter 2 or sections 72 to 75)

Preparing a care plan

06 For the time that a patient is subject to an interim CTO, it would be best practice to ensure, where the length of the interim order allows, that the patient's RMO draws up and implements a care plan with respect to that patient. Such a care plan would be as near as possible to any care plan prepared under section 76 of the Act where a patient is subject to a CTO.

Reviewing and revoking an interim CTO

07 In terms of section 72 of the Act, the patient's RMO is under a duty to keep the interim CTO under constant review. The RMO must revoke the order if at any point he/she is satisfied that:

- the patient no longer meets the criteria for compulsory powers which are set out at section 64(5)(a) to (d) of the Act; or
- it is no longer necessary for the patient to be subject to the interim CTO.

08 If the RMO revokes the interim CTO, he/she must give written notice of the fact along with a statement of his/her reasons for doing so to:

- the Commission;
- the patient;
- the patient's named person;
- any guardian of the patient;
- any welfare attorney of the patient;
- the patient's MHO; and
- the Tribunal.

09 The Commission also has the power to revoke an interim CTO if it is satisfied that the criteria for compulsory powers set out at section 73(2) are no longer satisfied. Where this happens, the Commission must give written notice of the fact along with a statement of its reasons for doing so to:

- the patient's RMO;
- the patient;
- the patient's named person;
- any guardian of the patient;
- any welfare attorney of the patient;
- the patient's MHO; and
- the Tribunal.

10 The Commission and the RMO must provide any such notification as soon as is practicable after revoking the interim CTO. Although they are under a duty to provide only written notice that the interim CTO has been revoked, it would be best practice for them to ensure, where practicable, that the patient and his/her representatives are informed verbally of the revocation as soon as possible. In other words, it would be best practice to ensure that the patient does not have to wait several days for the notification letter to arrive before being made aware of the fact that the order has in fact been revoked.

11 The Act imposes a duty on the RMO under section 74(1) to send a statement of reasons for the determination. The persons who must be given the information include the patient, their named person, any guardian, any welfare attorney, the MHO and the Tribunal. It will be for the RMO to consider in the circumstances what information is needed to meet the duty to give reasons and to provide that information whilst at the same time not providing information unnecessary or irrelevant to the determination which the patient is entitled to have kept confidential.

12 It would be expected that many of the parties listed at paragraphs 8 and 9 above would have been consulted prior to the decision being taken. For example, it would be expected that the patient's MHO would have been involved in the process leading up to the revocation to ensure that the likely impact of the removal of compulsory powers on the patient's social circumstances and home situation are given due consideration and the potential impact of any decision by the patient regarding self-discharge are given due consideration. Similarly, in order to comply with the duties laid out in section 1 of the Act, regard should be had to the views of any carers the patient may have with respect to a decision to revoke the order.

13 As with the revocation of any authority to detain under this Act, it would be best practice for the RMO, with the help of other members of the patient's multi-disciplinary team, to oversee the drawing up and implementation of a discharge plan of care where the patient is being discharged from hospital. This would also apply where the patient has been subject to community-based compulsory powers.

Responsibilities and best practice subsequent to the making of a CTO

RMO responsibilities: preparing the patient's care plan (section 76)

14 The patient's RMO must prepare a care plan setting out the forms of care and treatment for the mental disorder which are currently being given to the patient and which are proposed for the duration of the CTO. This care plan will be based very largely on the proposed care plan which was submitted to the Tribunal as part of the CTO application.

15 **The Mental Health (Content and amendment of care plans) (Scotland) Regulations 2005 (SSI No. 309)** ("the regulations") set out the information that must be contained in the care plan aside from the information detailed in paragraph 14 above. In general terms the regulations require that the following information must be detailed in the care plan;

(a) full details of the CTO and the day on which the order was made;
(b) the objectives of the medical treatment which it is proposed to give, and which is being given to the patient;
(c) details of any community care services or other relevant services and the objectives of those services which it is proposed to give, and which are being given to the patient;
(d) details of any other treatment, care or service (other than that described in section 76(2)(a) or in paragraph (c) above) and the objectives of that treatment, care or service which it is proposed to give, and which are being given, to the patient;
(e) the name and other appropriate contact details of the patient's responsible medical officer;
(f) the name and other appropriate contact details of the patient's mental health officer; and
(g) details of the 2 month period during which the statutory reviews under sections 77(2) or 78(2) are required to take place and the actual dates on which these reviews took place.

16 The full details of the CTO as referred to in paragraph 15(a) above would be the measures and any recorded matters authorised by the order.

17 With respect to the matters referred to in paragraph 15(g) above this simply means that when the care plan is first prepared under section 76(2) the RMO must detail on it the 2 month period during which the first statutory review must be carried out. When the first review has been

carried out and the RMO is updating the care plan as mentioned in paragraph 18 below he/she must include the date on which the review took place and then detail the 2 month period during which the next statutory review must be carried out and so on.

18 The regulations also specify the circumstances in which the RMO must amend the care plan. In general terms these are where:
(a) the Tribunal has made an order with respect to the CTO;
(b) the RMO has:
- made a determination extending the CTO under section 86(1);
- granted a certificate under:

(i) section 127(1) (b) which suspends the measure of detention in the CTO;
(ii) section 128(1) (b) which suspends other measures in the CTO; which specifies a period exceeding 28 days during which the patient's CTO shall not authorise the measure or measures specified in the certificate?
- revoked under section 129(2), a certificate granted under any of the powers referred to in the bullet point above; or
- carried out any further mandatory reviews of the CTO under section 78(2).

19 This care plan should be copied for the MHO, CPN and other members of the multi-disciplinary team providing care and treatment to the patient, including community care providers. A copy should also be given to the patient and the patient's named person.

20 Although section 76 of the Act places the duty on the RMO to draw up the care plan after the CTO has been made, the MHO (and the rest of the multi-disciplinary team) should contribute fully to the preparation of the finalised and agreed care plan. The RMO should consult widely with the multi-disciplinary team in any situation where the Tribunal panel has expressed a wish to see the proposed care plan significantly altered and/or has granted different compulsory measures from those sought in the original CTO application.

Local authority responsibilities: designating an MHO (section 229)

21 The Act places a duty on the relevant local authority to designate an MHO to be responsible for the patient's case as soon as is reasonably practicable after the CTO is made. In order to provide continuity of care, it would be best practice for the local authority to ensure that, where practicable, the MHO who is designated after the making of the CTO, is

the same MHO who made the CTO application. Local authorities should seek to minimise the number of changes in the designated MHO throughout the period to which the patient is subject to compulsory powers. The "relevant local authority" is defined in section 229(3) of the Act. *For further information on the process of designating an MHO, see Chapter 9 of Volume 1 of the Code of Practice.*

22 The designated MHO should take on the responsibility for ensuring that, as soon as is practicable after the CTO has been made, the patient and the patient's named person, independent advocate, family and carers as well as the members of the multi-disciplinary team, the relevant hospital managers and other legitimately interested parties are informed of his/her name and contact details. It would be best practice to ensure that this information is followed up in writing. The designated MHO should also ensure that, where practicable, the patient is seen in person as soon as possible after the CTO has been made. Such arrangements are particularly important in situations where:

- there has been a change of designated MHO between the application for the CTO being made and the order being made (even though such a change, as stated above, is undesirable);
- the CTO imposes community-based compulsory measures; and
- the patient was not subject to any form of compulsion immediately prior to the CTO being made.

23 It is important that the MHO's input into the patient's case does not lapse immediately or shortly after the CTO was made only to be revived at the time of a mandatory review several months later. This could necessitate, among other things, regular liaison with the patient's key workers and care managers, where appropriate. An MHO who is participating in a mandatory review of a CTO needs to have a well-informed and, preferably, first-hand view of the patient's recovery and progress since the CTO was made. The MHO should also ensure that he/she is involved with the periodic assessment and review of the care plan. This process of assessment and review could similarly be managed by way of local authority protocols. It would be best practice to ensure that the timing of this process is integrated with the RMO's responsibility to review the CTO 'from time to time'.

MHO responsibilities: preparing an SCR (section 231)

24 An MHO must prepare a Social Circumstances Report (SCR) within 21 days of the making of the CTO. As with all other occasions on which the duty to produce an SCR arises, the MHO may decide not to produce the SCR if he/she is satisfied that it would serve little or no practical purpose. *For further information on the SCR, see section 231 of the Act or Chapter 11 of Volume 1 of the Code of Practice.*

What should the various parties involved in the patient's care and treatment be doing on a day-to-day basis during the operation of the CTO?

25 The various parties of the patient's multi-disciplinary team (i.e. including voluntary sector service providers, allied health professionals, etc.) should work closely together to ensure and to monitor the provision of all the aspects of the care plan. The precise role to be played by each party in the multi-disciplinary team will necessarily be dictated by the specifics of the care plan. However, all members of the team should be fully involved in carrying out a range of duties (in addition to the duties imposed on them by the process of formally reviewing the CTO). Depending on the patient's level of need and personal circumstances, such duties could include:

- regularly exploring the continuing need for and the effectiveness of the compulsory powers granted by the Tribunal in relation to how the powers are being applied, and in relation to whether their ongoing application is justified;
- regularly exploring the extent to which the principles of the Act and other matters laid out at sections 1 to 3 of the Act are being respected; and
- keeping under regular review the extent to which the objectives of the care plan are being met and the extent to which the patient is being treated in the least restrictive environment possible.

26 All members of the patient's multi-disciplinary team should be pro-active in liaising with and reporting to one another with respect to the patient's condition. Each party should take responsibility for keeping the patient's MHO and RMO up to date with changes in the patient's condition and social circumstances. Doing so ensures that fully informed decisions can be made as to whether the CTO needs to be revoked or its compulsory measures and/or recorded matters varied. This is particularly important where the RMO and MHO do not have a substantial day-to-day involvement with the delivery of the care package. It would be best practice for reporting mechanisms and practices to be reviewed regularly by the patient's MHO and RMO.

Suspending the compulsory measures specified in a CTO or an ICTO (sections 127 to 129)

27 The patient's RMO can suspend any of the compulsory measures specified in a CTO. He/she can also suspend the hospital detention requirement specified in an ICTO. Section 127 of the Act, as amended by **The Mental Health (Care and Treatment (Scotland) Act 2003 (Modifications of Enactments) Order 2005**, of the Act and paragraphs 28 to 50 of this chapter deal with the suspension of the requirement to detain the patient in hospital. Section 128 and paragraphs 51 to 56 of this chapter examine the suspension of any of the other compulsory measures specified in a CTO. Finally, paragraphs 57 to 61 examine the issue of revoking a suspension certificate which is addressed in the Act at section 129.

Suspension of hospital detention requirement where a patient is subject to a CTO or an ICTO (section 127)

28 Where a patient is subject to a CTO or an ICTO which specifies that the patient be detained in hospital, it is possible to suspend that hospital detention requirement for a limited period of time (and thereby suspend the patient's detention in hospital) without revoking the order in its entirety. Under such circumstances, section 127(1) of the Act allows for a "suspension certificate" to be granted. Such a certificate can only be granted by the patient's RMO.

How long does a suspension certificate last?

29 In terms of section 127(1) of the Act, the suspension certificate can last for any period of time as long as this period is not greater than 6 months if the patient is subject to a CTO. Where the patient is subject to an ICTO, the suspension certificate can last for any period of time, in terms of section 127(3), as amended, of the Act. In both cases, the expiry date of the suspension certificate must not go beyond the proposed expiry date of the CTO or the ICTO. In terms of section 127(4), the period specified in a suspension certificate may be the duration of an event or series of events with or without any associated travel.

30 There are additional considerations with respect to timescales where a patient is subject to a CTO. The RMO may not grant a suspension certificate if the period authorised in that suspension certificate, when taken together with any other suspension certificate granted in respect of that patient, would be greater than 9 months within the 12 month period which would end with the expiry of the proposed suspension certificate. This is to prevent a patient being subject to suspension certificates for unnecessarily long periods of time.

Can conditions be attached to the suspension certificate?

31 Yes. The patient's RMO may by virtue of section 127(5) and (6) of the Act attach certain conditions to the certificate irrespective of whether the patient is subject to a hospital-based CTO or ICTO. These conditions are:

- that the patient be kept in the charge of a person authorised in writing for that purpose by the patient's RMO; and
- any other conditions as may be specified by the patient's RMO.

32 The reasons which must motivate the attaching of conditions to a suspension certificate are set out in section 127(5) of the Act. They are that:

- it is necessary in the interests of the patient to do so; or
- it is necessary for the protection of any other person to do so.

33 It should be noted that the RMO's giving of authority to another person to keep a patient in his/her charge can only be done in writing.

34 Examples of conditions which could be attached to a suspension certificate include that the patient live in a specified place under the care of a specified person; be kept in the charge of an escorting nurse; or that the patient accept visits from a medical practitioner or an MHO. It would be best practice for the RMO to ensure that the patient's MHO and other members of the multi-disciplinary team are informed of any conditions attached to the suspension certificate, and to ensure that procedures and contingency plans are put in place for any occasion where the conditions are not complied with.

35 When attaching conditions to a suspension certificate, the patient's RMO should also consider the extent to which it would be more appropriate to make an application to the Tribunal under section 95 of the Act seeking a variation of the CTO.

When would it be appropriate to grant a suspension certificate?

36 A suspension certificate suspending the hospital detention requirement could be granted for a number of reasons including a compassionate visit or emergency treatment in another hospital, as described below. Its main purpose, however, will be to act as a tool in the process of planning a patient's discharge from compulsory measures and, more generally, from in-patient psychiatric services. For example, a suspension certificate could be granted to allow the patient to visit and/or be assessed in a place likely to be providing a community care service; or to allow the patient to be gradually re-integrated into their pre-existing social circumstances in the community. This could include allowing the patient to make visits to home or to stay overnight at home, with relatives and carers, or in other care facilities.

37 The patient's RMO should give full consideration to the need for a multi-disciplinary assessment of the impact on health and welfare of the patient and others, of the proposed stay in the community. Any proposed suspension of detention and its objectives should concord fully with the patient's agreed care plan and its objectives. In coming to a conclusion on the appropriateness of the proposed suspension certificate, it will be vitally important that the RMO involve the patient's MHO and other members of the multi-disciplinary team fully. All practitioners involved in this process should also have regard to the principles of the Act and other matters laid out in sections 1 to 3, when deciding whether or not to grant a suspension certificate. Particularly important among these principles, is the principle stated at section 1(4) of the Act which provides for any person discharging a function under the Act to discharge that function in a manner which "involves the minimum restriction on the freedom of the patient that is necessary in the circumstances".

38 It would be expected that the patient and the patient's named person be as fully involved as possible with the planning process preceding the decision to grant a suspension certificate. Subject to the patient's consent, detailed prior consultation will also need to take place with any appropriate relatives or friends of the patient (particularly where the patient is to reside with them once no longer detained in hospital) and with relevant community service providers. It would be best practice not to grant a suspension certificate where the patient does not consent to relatives or friends being consulted, where they are to be involved in his/her care once no longer in hospital.

39 The patient's RMO, in consultation with the patient's multi-disciplinary team, will need to give careful consideration to whether the compulsory measures specified in a patient's CTO should in fact be varied under section 95 of the Act rather than temporarily suspended, before taking the final decision to grant a suspension certificate. While there will undoubtedly be occasions when it is appropriate to grant a suspension certificate as a means of assessing the patient's likely recovery in a community environment rather than in a hospital, a suspension certificate should not be granted merely as a means of avoiding the need to make a section 95 application to the Tribunal to vary a CTO or of avoiding discharging the patient from compulsory measures altogether. For example, attaching a condition to a suspension certificate which stipulates that the patient reside at a specified place should not be used as a long-term alternative to applying to the Tribunal for an order which would vary a previously hospital-based CTO to a community-based CTO which specifies a residence requirement. Accordingly, a suspension certificate and the extent to which it is meeting its objectives should be kept under constant review by the patient's multi-disciplinary team with a view either to revoking the CTO or to making an application to the Tribunal to vary the compulsory measures specified in the order as soon as either option becomes appropriate.

40 Particular consideration should be given to the need for an application under section 95 of the Act where any of the conditions attached to the suspension certificate are equivalent to any community-based compulsory measures which were not discussed and considered by the Tribunal when the CTO was first made.

41 The decision as to whether to proceed with the granting of a suspension certificate as an alternative to an application under section 95 of the Act will ultimately depend on the extent to which the multi-disciplinary team is confident that the patient is ready to be discharged to the community. If the multi-disciplinary team have reservations about the patient's readiness to be discharged, it would be appropriate to grant a suspension certificate which would make the patient's stay in the community subject to an early review. Such a review should be undertaken sooner rather than later after the suspension certificate was granted with a view to making a section 95 application to the Tribunal.

42 A suspension certificate should only be granted under sections 127 or 128 of the Act where it accords with the assessed needs of the patient and not as a means of managing beds in wards which are running at or above capacity. A decision to suspend the power to detain a patient in hospital should only be taken where it is in the best interests of the patient.

Who is responsible for the patient's care and treatment while subject to a suspension certificate?

43 The patient's RMO remains responsible for the patient's care and treatment while the patient is subject to a suspension certificate. He/she must therefore ensure that appropriate arrangements are made for the patient's care and treatment while not in hospital. It should also be remembered that the duty under section 1(6) of the Act to provide "appropriate services" to the patient includes any time where the patient is subject to a suspension certificate.

44 It is important that the patient's relatives and carers (especially where the patient is residing with them for the duration of the suspension certificate) and all the members of the patient's multi-disciplinary team should have clear lines of communication with the patient's RMO so that the patient's progress towards recovery can be effectively monitored and acted upon, where appropriate.

45 Where the duration of the suspension certificate is fairly lengthy (for example, for more than 28 days), it would be best practice for the patient's RMO to issue a written reminder to the patient to return to hospital shortly before the period of suspension is due to end. If the patient does not return on time, then he/she can be said to have absconded and may be dealt with in terms of Part 20 of the Act.

Who must be notified prior to the granting of a suspension certificate?

46 There are a range of notification procedures attached to the granting of a suspension certificate under section 127 of the Act. These are set out in subsections (7) to (9) of that section. If the hospital detention requirement is to be suspended for a period of more than 28 days, the RMO must give notice of the proposal to suspend the CTO to the following parties:

- the patient
- the patient's named person;
- the patient's general medical practitioner; and
- the patient's mental health officer.

47 It should be noted that the RMO must provide notification to these parties before the suspension certificate under section 127(1) is granted. The RMO must additionally give notice to the Commission of the granting of a suspension certificate specifying a period of more than 28 days within 14 days of it being granted.

48 It would be best practice to ensure that these parties receive similar notifications where a suspension period of less than 28 days is proposed.

What should happen where a patient requires emergency treatment in another hospital?

49 There may be rare occasions where a patient who is detained in hospital on the authority of a CTO or an ICTO requires to be transferred urgently to another hospital to receive emergency treatment for a physical disorder. If there is insufficient time in such circumstances to effect a formal transfer of the patient under Part 7, Chapter 6 of the Act, it would be permissible to grant a suspension certificate suspending the hospital detention requirement of the CTO or the ICTO as this would allow the transfer of the patient to take place urgently. It should be remembered, however, that the patient could not be detained in the second hospital (i.e. the patient could not be prevented from leaving that hospital) given that the first hospital will be explicitly specified in the CTO. The patient could only be detained in the second hospital where the patient's RMO has explicitly cited residence in the second hospital as a condition of the suspension certificate.

50 Best practice would suggest that the RMO should take steps to ensure that the patient's named person, primary carer, MHO and other relevant members of the multi-disciplinary team are informed of any emergency transfer as soon as possible after it becomes apparent that the transfer may be necessary.

Can a suspension certificate be granted with respect to compulsory measures other than the hospital detention requirement? (section 128)

51 Yes. Section 128 of the Act permits the patient's RMO to grant a suspension certificate suspending any compulsory measure specified in a CTO other than the hospital detention requirement. Compulsory measures other than the hospital detention requirement cannot be suspended where the patient is subject to an ICTO.

52 It should also be noted that a patient's RMO cannot attach conditions to a suspension certificate granted under section 128. This is in contrast to a suspension certificate granted under section 127 which suspends the hospital detention requirement where the patient is subject to a CTO or an ICTO.

53 The reasons for granting such a suspension certificate will be similar to those motivating the granting of a suspension certificate which suspends the hospital detention requirement of a CTO or ICTO. For further information on this point, see paragraphs 31 to 35 of this chapter.

54 A suspension certificate granted under section 128(1) of the Act may not last longer than 3 months. The RMO may not grant a suspension certificate if the period authorised in that certificate, when taken together with any other suspension certificate suspending compulsory measures other than the hospital detention requirement, would be greater than 3 months.

55 Before granting a suspension certificate under section 128(1) of the Act, in terms of section 128(4), the patient's RMO must notify the following parties of the compulsory measures to be suspended; the period for which they are to be suspended; and the RMO's reasons for suspending them. The parties to be notified are:

- the patient;
- the patient's named person; and
- the patient's mental health officer.

56 The RMO must provide notification to these parties *before* the suspension certificate is granted under section 128(1). In terms of section 128(5), the RMO must additionally within 14 days of the suspension certificate being granted, give notice to the Commission of the granting of the certificate; the measures suspended by the certificate and the period for which they are to be suspended; and the RMO's reasons for suspending those measures. It would always be best practice to ensure that any such notifications are provided as soon as possible after the duty to provide them arises.

Can a suspension certificate be revoked?

57 Any suspension certificate granted under sections 127(1), 127(3) or 128(1) of the Act can be revoked by the patient's RMO under section 129 if he/she is satisfied that it is necessary in the interests of the patient to do so or that it is necessary for the protection of any other person to do so.

58 In terms of section 129(3), as soon as practicable after revoking a certificate which suspended the hospital detention requirement of a CTO or ICTO, the RMO must notify the following parties of the revocation. The parties are:

- the patient;
- the patient's named person;
- the patient's mental health officer;
- any person who was authorised to keep the patient in their charge during the period authorised by the suspension certificate; and
- the patient's general medical practitioner.

59 It would be expected, however, that the RMO discuss with the patient and the other parties mentioned in the preceding paragraph any possible revocation of the suspension certificate before the certificate is suspended. The RMO should, for example, consider very carefully the reasons for revoking the certificate and, in particular, the effects this revocation might have on the patient's recovery.

60 In terms of section 129(4), as soon as practicable after revoking a suspension certificate which suspended any compulsory measure specified in a CTO other than the hospital detention requirement, the RMO must notify the following parties of the revocation and of the reasons for revoking it. The parties are the patient; the patient's named person; and the patient's mental health officer.

61 Where any suspension certificate is revoked, the patient's RMO must notify the Commission of the revocation within 14 days of it having taken place in terms of section 129(5).

chapter 5

reviewing a compulsory treatment order (part 7, chapter 4 or sections 77 to 111)

chapter five

Introduction

This chapter examines the formal processes to be followed where a CTO is being reviewed, as laid out in Part 7 Chapter 4 of the Act. It explores, firstly, the duty placed on a patient's RMO to keep under review the continuing need for compulsory powers as well as the occasions on which he/she is under a duty to carry out a formal or mandatory review of the CTO. The possible outcomes of these reviews are that:

- a CTO could be revoked;
- a CTO could be extended with no variation of the compulsory measures or recorded matters specified in the order;
- a CTO could be extended with a variation of the compulsory measures or recorded matters specified in the order; and
- the compulsory measures or recorded matters specified in a CTO could be varied.

The procedures which must be followed with respect to each of these outcomes are discussed in sections 77 to 95 of the Act or paragraphs 5 to 85 of this chapter. These procedures are also illustrated by a range of flowcharts which can be found on pages 129, 136, 146 and 154.

Sections 96 to 100 of the Act or paragraphs 86 to 113 of this chapter then look at a range of other applications which can be made to the Tribunal with respect to a CTO. These are:

- the RMO's duty to make a reference to the Tribunal where a recorded matter specified in a CTO is not being provided;
- the Commission's power to make a reference to the Tribunal;
- the patient's or the patient's named person's right to make an application to the Tribunal to revoke a section 86 determination to extend a CTO; and
- the patient's or the patient's named person's right to make an application to the Tribunal to revoke a CTO or to vary the terms of a CTO.

chapter five

Overview of the review process

What are the criteria which should be used when reviewing the CTO?

01 The criteria against which a patient's mental health must be judged when any review of a CTO is taking place are set out in section 77(3)(b) of the Act and are modelled on the criteria for granting the CTO which are set out in section 64(5)(a) to (d). The criteria are:

- that the person has a mental disorder;
- that medical treatment which would be likely to prevent the mental disorder from worsening or to alleviate any of the symptoms, or effect of the disorder, is available for the person;
- that, if the person were not provided with this medical treatment, there would be a significant risk to the health, safety or welfare of the person or to the safety of any other person;
- that, because of the person's mental disorder, their decision-making ability in respect of that medical treatment is significantly impaired; and
- that it continues to be necessary for the person to be subject to a compulsory treatment order.

02 When assessing whether the patient still meets these criteria for compulsory powers, the RMO must bear in mind that it is his/her responsibility to demonstrate that the criteria are met. In other words, the presumption is always in favour of revoking the CTO unless the RMO is satisfied that the criteria are met. The onus is not therefore on the patient to demonstrate that he/she no longer meets the criteria.

03 In assessing the patient against these criteria, the RMO should be fully supported by all members of the multi-disciplinary team who are involved in providing care, support and treatment to the patient. This is particularly important where the patient is subject to a community-based CTO and/or where the RMO does not have a substantial day-to-day involvement in the patient's care. Where this is the case, it is the responsibility of the members of the multi-disciplinary team to provide the RMO and other members of the team with regular updates on the patient's progress towards recovery and on the extent to which the objectives of the care plan are being met. It is also the responsibility of the RMO to seek information on the patient's condition from other members of the multi-disciplinary team.

04 The key consideration for the RMO when assessing the patient against the relevant criteria for compulsory powers is whether the care and treatment set out in the patient's care plan which are being provided on a compulsory basis do in fact still require to be provided on a compulsory basis. The assessment should thus focus on whether the care plan continues to represent the least restrictive environment in which the patient can safely be provided with beneficial care and treatment. Any such assessment should evaluate the potential risks to the mental health and welfare of the patient and of others if the elements of compulsion in the care plan were no longer to be provided on a compulsory basis. However, it would, in general, not be acceptable to justify the continued recourse to a CTO solely on the basis that the patient, once no longer subject to the compulsory measures authorised by the CTO, might revert to activities which could be detrimental to his/her mental health and welfare. A CTO should not be continued on the basis of a preventative function alone: it should only be continued where the RMO is satisfied that the criteria listed at section 83(2)(a) and (b) of the Act continue to be met with respect to the patient.

chapter five

Carrying out a review – What must be done and when?

05 The Act places a duty on the patient's RMO to review a CTO on two separate sets of occasions. The RMO must:
- carry out "mandatory reviews" of a CTO; and
- review a CTO "from time to time".

06 Paragraphs 7 to 11 of this chapter examine the processes involved in carrying out a mandatory review while paragraphs 12 to 15 examine those connected with a "from time to time review". Paragraphs 16 to 17 look at the possible outcomes of these reviews.

Mandatory reviews (sections 77 and 78)

07 A mandatory review must be carried out during the 2 month period which ends with the day on which the CTO is due to expire. It should be noted that a CTO lasts for 6 months from when it was first made, then for a further 6 months if extended, after which it may be extended for a further 12 months and thereafter every 12 months. In addition therefore to the mandatory review which must be carried out before the expiry of the first 6 month period of compulsory powers authorised by the CTO, the RMO must also carry out "further mandatory reviews" . These must be carried out during the 2 month period which ends with the day on which the CTO is due to expire after having been extended by way of:
- a section 86 determination to extend a CTO; and
- an order made by the Tribunal under section 103 of the Act (such an order could be made subsequent to a section 92 application to extend and vary the CTO, a section 95 application to vary the CTO or applications by the patient or the named person under sections 99 and 100).

08 The steps which the RMO must take when carrying out any mandatory review are set out in section 77(3) to (5) of the Act. These are:
- to carry out a medical examination of the patient (or arrange for another approved medical practitioner to examine the patient);
- to consider whether the patient continues to meet the criteria for compulsory powers, as referred to at section 77(3)(b) of the Act and paragraph 1 above;
- to consult the patient's MHO;
- to consult the persons who appear to the RMO to provide to the patient the medical treatment, community care services or other relevant services which are set out in the patient's care plan; and

- to consult any other persons whom the RMO deems to be appropriate (for example, any carers the patient may have).

09 It would always be best practice for the patient's RMO to carry out the medical examination forming part of the mandatory review rather than another approved medical practitioner, where this proves to be practicable.

10 It is important to bear in mind that the RMO must test whether it is necessary for the patient to be subject to a CTO. In other words, a particularly important aspect of any review is to test whether compulsory powers are still required and whether appropriate care and treatment could be given to the patient with the patient's consent.

11 The process of carrying out a mandatory review should be characterised from beginning to end by as great a sense of multi-agency and multi-disciplinary co-operation and consultation as is practicable. In that connection, it would be best practice for a full case conference to be held when a mandatory review is being carried out. This will be particularly important where the patient's RMO has had only limited active involvement in the day-to-day care management and delivery of the care plan, as could be the case with respect to a community-based patient. It would also be best practice to use the opportunity presented by the mandatory review to review not only whether the patient still meets the criteria for compulsory powers but also whether the various reporting mechanisms which have been in operation throughout the period of compulsory powers authorised by the CTO are operating effectively.

Other reviews of "from time to time reviews" (section 80)

12 The RMO should carry out "from time to time" reviews as frequently as is practicable. Although it is difficult, by definition, to place a precise timetable on when such reviews should take place, they should not necessarily be seen as formal reviews which are separate from the simple day-to-day monitoring of the patient's progress towards recovery. Existing multi-disciplinary or multi-agency forums, such as ward rounds, planned out-patient visits to a day hospital or NHS resource centre could all, be seen as appropriate settings for a "from time to time" review. The fact that such a review has taken place should always be noted alongside any other matters routinely noted at such meetings.

13 Although the Act does not place a formal duty on the RMO to consult with, for example, the patient's MHO, other members of the patient's multi-disciplinary team or the patient's carers, during this 'from time to time' review process, it would always be best practice for the RMO to remain in close consultation with these parties as regularly as is practicable for the duration of the CTO. The importance of such regular contact with all relevant parties is to enable the RMO to be in full possession of all the relevant information (including the social circumstances dimension for which the MHO has responsibility) when assessing the extent to which the care plan's objectives are being met.

14 It is also important that such consultation process is seen as a dynamic two-way process. Other members of the multi-disciplinary team and, where relevant, other carers of the patient should feel free to and should be able to, contact the RMO with relevant information wherever they deem it appropriate.

15 While the Act places the responsibility on the patient's RMO for carrying out "from time to time" reviews, it would be expected that the continuing need for a CTO would also be monitored on a daily basis by all the parties providing care and treatment to the patient. These parties should be engaging with the RMO as well as with the other members of the multi-disciplinary team providing care, treatment and support to the patient to ensure that the order is monitored and reviewed effectively.

chapter five

Options Subsequent to a Review Taking Place

16 After having complied with the review duties imposed by the Act and after having had regard to the views of those parties as required by the Act, a number of possibilities are open to the RMO. The RMO could:

- revoke the CTO by way of sections 79 and 80;
- extend the CTO by way of a determination under section 86;
- apply to the Tribunal for extension of the CTO and variation of the compulsory measures or recorded matters specified in the order under section 92 of the Act where he/she has carried out a mandatory review; or
- apply to the Tribunal under section 95 for variation of the compulsory measures or recorded matters specified in the CTO where he/she has carried out a "from time to time" review.

17 The possible outcomes of mandatory and "from time to time" reviews are illustrated below.

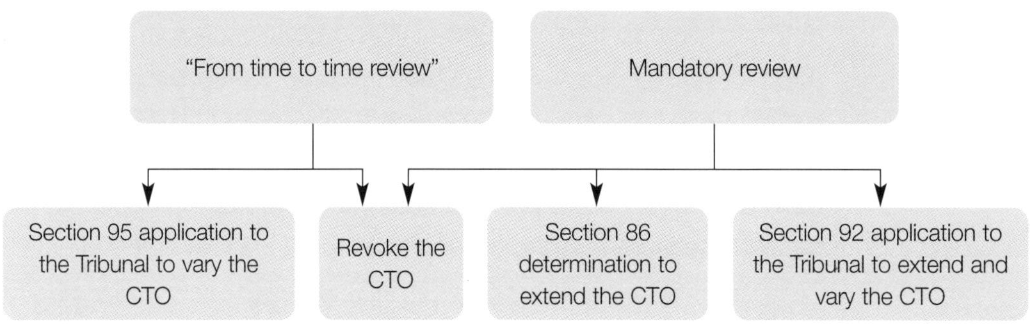

Revoking the CTO

When must a CTO be revoked? (sections 79, 80 & 82)

18 The patient's RMO must make a determination revoking the CTO where one or more of the 2 following conditions are met:

- where the RMO is not satisfied that the conditions mentioned in section 64(5)(a) to (d) of the Act continue to be met in respect of the patient. (Note that these conditions are discussed above in paragraphs 1 to 4 of this chapter.)
- where the RMO is not satisfied that it continues to be necessary for the patient to be subject to the CTO (that is, the RMO is satisfied that the patient does not need to be subject to compulsory powers and will accept treatment voluntarily).

19 The patient's RMO must make a determination revoking the CTO as soon as practicable after being satisfied that one or more of the two conditions above are met. If either of these conditions is met, the RMO should not simply allow the CTO to expire on its renewal date (which could be, for example, several weeks away) but should always comply with the relevant statutory procedures for revoking the CTO and notifying the relevant parties as soon as is practicable.

Whom must the RMO notify of the determination to revoke the CTO? (section 82)

20 Where the RMO decides to revoke a CTO, either as a result of a mandatory review or a 'from time to time' review, he/she must notify a range of parties of this decision. This notification must be accompanied by a statement of the reasons for the revocation. It is recommended that form REV2 be used for this purpose. The parties which the Act states must be notified are:

- the patient;
- the patient's named person;
- any guardian of the patient;
- any welfare attorney of the patient;
- the patient's MHO;
- the Tribunal; and
- the Commission.

21 The patient, the named person, and any guardian or welfare attorney must be notified as soon as is practicable after the decision to revoke the CTO has been made and in any event within 7 days. Notification to the MHO, the Tribunal and the Commission must be given within 7 days of the making of the determination to revoke the CTO. The RMO should also bear in mind that these parties might not receive this written notice for several days. Best practice would therefore dictate that those parties be informed verbally as soon as is possible after making the determination.

The Commission's power to revoke a CTO (section 81)

22 The Commission has the power to revoke a CTO where it is satisfied that the conditions mentioned in section 64(5) for compulsory powers are no longer met or that it is no longer necessary for the patient to be subject to a CTO. Where the Commission makes such a determination, it must give notice of its decision and send a statement of its reasons to:

- the patient;
- the patient's named person;
- any guardian and any welfare attorney of the patient;
- the patient's MHO;
- the patient's RMO; and
- the Tribunal.

23 If the Commission revokes a CTO, it must notify the patient, the named person and any guardian and welfare attorney of the patient as soon as is practicably possible of its decision to revoke the order and in any event within 7 days. It must also notify the patient's RMO, the patient's MHO and the Tribunal, within 7 days.

24 Where the patient is to be discharged from compulsory powers when the CTO is revoked either by the RMO or by the Commission, the RMO should oversee arrangements for the drawing up and putting into practice of a coherent and comprehensive discharge plan of care. This will enable the RMO and the multi-disciplinary team to comply with the duty placed on them by way of section 1(6) of the Act to "have regard to the importance of the provision of appropriate services to the person who is, or has been, subject to a [CTO]".

What happens where the RMO decides not to revoke the CTO?

25 After reviewing a CTO, the RMO may decide not to revoke the order. At this point, section 83(3) of the Act places the RMO under a duty to:

- assess the needs of the patient for medical treatment for mental disorder;
- consider whether the CTO should be extended beyond the day on which it is due to expire;
- consider whether any of the compulsory measures or recorded matters specified in the CTO need to be varied and what modification is appropriate; and
- consider any views on these above three matters which may be expressed by the parties listed at section 77(3)(c) of the Act.

26 The parties listed at section 77(3)(c) of the Act are:

- the patient's MHO;
- any persons that the RMO considers appropriate to consult among those who provide medical treatment, community care services or relevant services, and any other treatment, care or service to the patient as set out in the care plan; and
- any other persons that the RMO considers appropriate.

27 In effect, the RMO is being asked to review the objectives of the patient's care plan; the extent to which those objectives are being met; if they are not being met in full, the reasons why they are not being met and whether any changes to the compulsory measures or recorded matters specified in the order need to be sought in order to realise the objectives of the care plan.

28 As a result of these deliberations, the RMO has three options with respect to the patient's CTO depending on whether a mandatory review or a "from time to time" review has taken place. These are:

- the CTO can be extended without any variation of the compulsory measures or recorded matters it specifies where a mandatory review has been carried out. If the RMO chooses this option, he/she must make a "section 86 determination". This option is explored in paragraphs 31 to 43 of this chapter.

- the CTO can be extended with a variation of the compulsory measures or recorded matters specified where a mandatory review has been carried out. If the RMO chooses this option, he/she must make an application to the Tribunal under section 92. This option is explored in paragraphs 49 to 69 of this chapter.
- the compulsory measures or recorded matters specified in the order can be varied. If the RMO chooses this option, he/she will need to make an application to the Tribunal under section 95. This option only applies where the RMO has carried out a "from time to time review" not if he/she has carried out a mandatory review. This option is explored in paragraphs 70 to 85 of this chapter.

29 These three options and the resulting decisions which the Tribunal can make are illustrated by the flowchart on page 129.

chapter five

CTO REVIEW PROCESS (PART 7, CHAPTER 4)

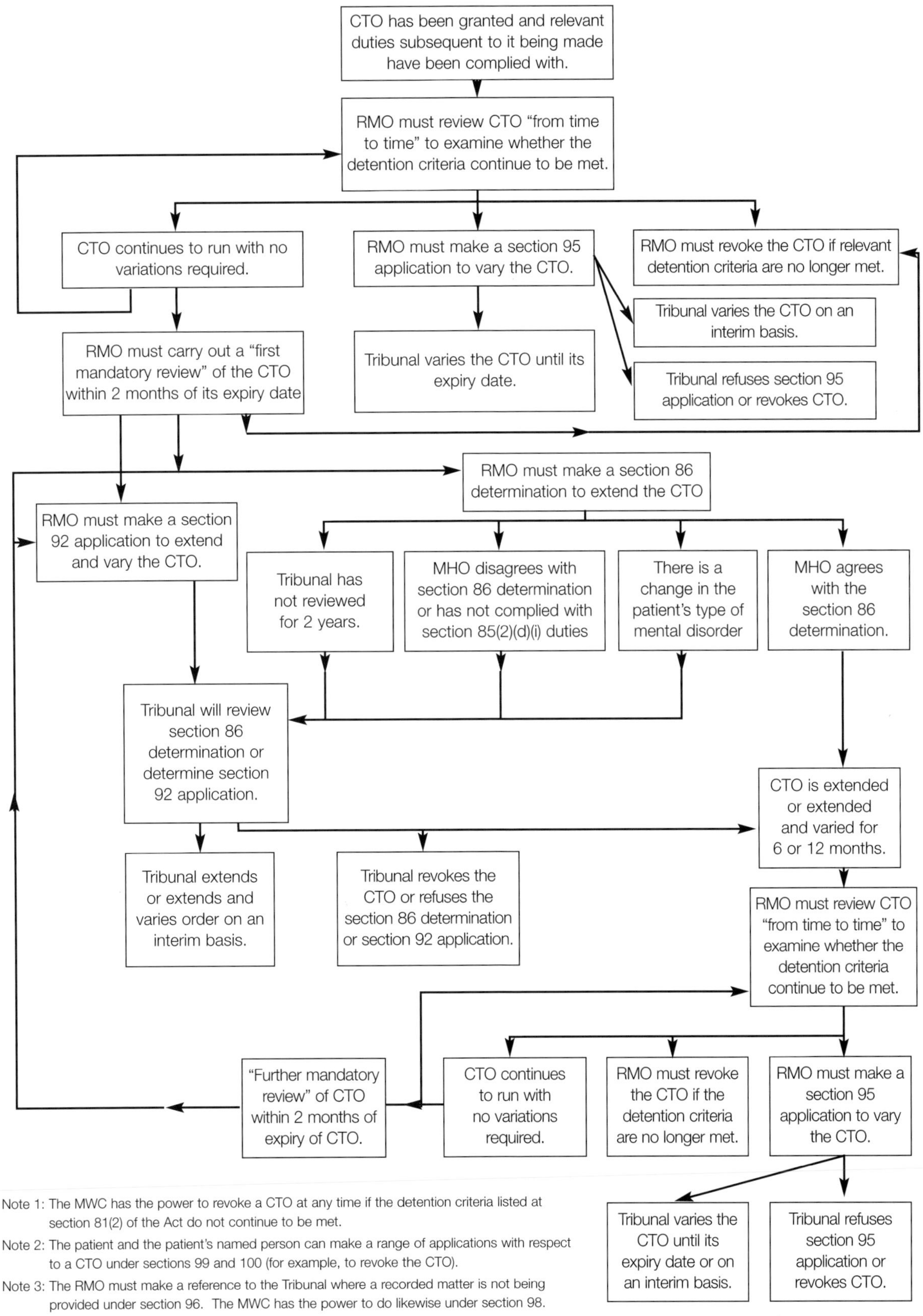

Note 1: The MWC has the power to revoke a CTO at any time if the detention criteria listed at section 81(2) of the Act do not continue to be met.

Note 2: The patient and the patient's named person can make a range of applications with respect to a CTO under sections 99 and 100 (for example, to revoke the CTO).

Note 3: The RMO must make a reference to the Tribunal where a recorded matter is not being provided under section 96. The MWC has the power to do likewise under section 98.

Extending the CTO without a variation of its terms: "A section 86 determination"

30 Where the RMO decides that the CTO should be extended beyond the day on which it is due to expire, he/she must make a determination under section 86 of the Act to extend the CTO. The CTO can be extended by 6 months initially, then by a further 12 months, then 12 monthly thereafter. The flowchart on page 136 illustrates the process of making a section 86 determination.

Notification in advance of making the determination (sections 84 and 85)

31 Before the RMO can make a section 86 determination to extend the CTO, he/she must give notice to the patient's MHO that he/she intends to make such a determination. The RMO will need to issue this notification well in advance of the expiry of the CTO given that the MHO must comply with a range of duties before the order can be extended. It is therefore advisable that the RMO ensures that the MHO has received this written notification at least 2 weeks before the CTO is due to expire.

32 Upon being notified of the RMO's intention to make a section 86 determination, the MHO must carry out a range of duties. These duties are:

- to interview the patient, except where it is impracticable to do so;
- to inform the patient that the RMO is proposing to extend the CTO for either 6 or 12 months;
- to inform the patient of his/her rights in relation to the section 86 determination;
- to inform the patient of the availability of independent advocacy services;
- to take appropriate steps to ensure that the patient has the opportunity to make use of those independent advocacy services;
- to inform the RMO of whether he/she agrees with the determination to extend the order; and, if he/she disagrees, the reasons for that disagreement; and
- to inform the RMO of any other matters which he/she considers to be relevant.

33 These MHO duties have a triple purpose. First, it is to ensure that the patient is as aware of the proposals as possible and able to exercise his/her rights with respect to the proposals (for example, so that he/she can make an appeal under section 99 to revoke a section 86 determination). Second, it is to evaluate the effectiveness of the care plan and the extent to which its objectives are being met. The MHO will also need to assess the likely continuing effectiveness of the order. Third, it is to assess the extent to which the patient is likely to accept treatment on a voluntary rather than compulsory basis.

34 It should be noted that many of the duties described above are similar to those which an MHO must carry out when making an application for a CTO and many of the duties applicable there are relevant here too. *(For best practice guidance with respect to these duties, see Chapter 5 of this Volume of the Code of Practice.)* It would therefore be expected that the MHO would attach the same degree of importance and effort to, for example, helping the patient access independent advocacy services upon being notified of the RMO's intention to make a section 86 determination as he/she would during the CTO application process.

35 At section 87(2)(a)(iii), the Act raises the possibility of the MHO not complying with the duty to inform the RMO of his/her opinion. However, there are in reality very few conceivable situations in which an MHO should not be able to comply with this duty. If, for reasons of practicability, the MHO is unable to comply with the duty within the prescribed timescales, the relevant local authority's MHO service should ensure that an alternative MHO provides the required assessment.

The RMO must make a "section 86 determination": i.e. prepare a record of the decision to extend the CTO

36 Before finally making the section 86 determination, the RMO is under a duty to have regard to the views of the patient's MHO as well as to the views of any providers of care, treatment or services which are set out in the patient's care plan. The RMO must also have regard to the principles of the Act and the other matters set out in sections 1 to 3. Of particular importance in this respect is the duty to have regard to the views of the patient's named person, carers, guardian and/or welfare attorney.

37 If, after having had regard to all those views, the RMO is still satisfied that the CTO should be extended without a variation of its terms, then he/she must make a determination to extend the order by 6 months, if the order has not already been extended, or by 12 months, if the order has already been in operation for 12 months or more. The RMO must then prepare a record of his determination in terms of section 87(2). It is recommended that form CTO3a be used for this purpose. This must be prepared as soon as is practicable after he/she has made the determination to extend the CTO.

38 The RMO's record of the section 86 determination must:

- state the reasons for the determination to extend the CTO;
- contain a statement of whether the MHO agrees or disagrees with the determination to extend the order. If the MHO does disagree, the RMO must state the MHO's reasons for disagreeing. Alternatively, the RMO can state that the MHO has not expressed any opinion as to whether the order should be extended; and
- contain a statement as to the type(s) of mental disorder that the patient has. (These types of mental disorder are set out at section 328(1) of the Act. They are: mental illness, personality disorder, and learning disability.) If there has been any change in the type(s) of mental disorder which the patient has from the type(s) which the patient had when the CTO was first made, then the RMO must state this too.

39 This record must then be submitted to:

- the Tribunal;
- the patient;
- the patient's named person;
- the patient's MHO; and
- the Commission.

40 Section 87(2)(c) of the Act gives the RMO the right to withhold a copy of this record from the patient. However, he/she may only do so where he/she believes that sending him/her a copy would create a risk of significant harm to the patient or to others. The RMO must state on the record whether or not he/she will be providing the patient with a copy of the record. If a copy is being withheld, the record must contain a statement of the reasons for not giving the patient a copy.

chapter five

41 There may be occasions on which there is a difference of professional opinion between members of the multi-disciplinary team with respect to the RMO's determination to extend the CTO under section 86 of the Act. One example could be where the RMO wishes to extend the CTO without a variation of its compulsory measures or recorded matters even though a clinical psychologist providing a psychological intervention to the patient, which is a recorded matter, is not satisfied that that psychological intervention remains appropriate or necessary.

42 In such a case, where the RMO and psychologist remain unable to resolve their difference of opinion, it would be expected that the psychologist would bring his/her views to the attention of the patient's MHO who has the right to formally disagree with the RMO's determination to extend the order. (Whether the MHO does exercise that right would be for the MHO to decide after consultation with the psychologist concerned, the RMO and other members of the multi-disciplinary team.) Where the MHO exercises this right, the Tribunal must review the CTO in terms of section 101(2)(a)(ii) of the Act. It would then be for the Tribunal to resolve this difference in professional opinion by determining whether or not the CTO should be extended and/or whether or not any recorded matter specified in the order should be varied. (Further information on the occasions when the Tribunal will review a section 86 determination can be found in section 101 of the Act and in paragraph 44 of this chapter.)

43 An alternative course of action in the above example (and one which is likely to represent the option of last resort) where those differences of professional opinion remain unresolved, would be for the psychologist to bring his/her views to the attention of the Mental Welfare Commission. The Commission has the power under section 98 of the Act to make a reference to the Tribunal on any subject. On receipt of such a reference, the Tribunal could make an order under section 104 of the Act varying any of the compulsory measures or recorded matters specified in the CTO.

Will the Tribunal always review the RMO's section 86 determination? (section 101)

44 The Tribunal need not always review the RMO's decision to make a section 86 determination. Section 101 of the Act sets out the circumstances when the Tribunal shall review the determination. These are:

- if, in the RMO's record submitted to the Tribunal, there is a difference between, on the one hand, the type(s) of mental disorder set out in that record, and, on the other, the type(s) of mental disorder recorded in the CTO;
- if the MHO disagrees with the RMO's determination;
- if the MHO has failed to inform the RMO whether he/she agrees or disagrees with the RMO's determination; and
- if a Tribunal hearing has not been held with respect to that patient's CTO within the last 2 years (i.e. within the period of 2 years finishing with the day on which the CTO would be due to expire if not otherwise extended).

Does the Tribunal require any other documents where it is reviewing a section 86 determination?

45 Yes. **The Mental Health (Compulsory Treatment Orders – Documents and Reports to be submitted to the Tribunal (Scotland) Regulations 2005 (SSI No. 366)** ("the regulations") provide that if the Tribunal is of the view it has insufficient information to make a decision, the regulations provide that it may require the patient's MHO to prepare and submit a report which should include the following details:

- the steps taken by the MHO in pursuance of with the requirements of the MHO's duties to the patient under section 85(2);
- the views of the MHO on the determination and reasons for these;
- the patient's views and those of the patient's named person, and reason for those views if known to the MHO;
- relevant details of the patient's personal circumstances;
- details of any advance statement made by the patient (and not withdrawn) if known; and
- any other information the MHO deems of assistance to the Tribunal in considering the determination.

Who must be given the opportunity to make representation to the Tribunal where a section 86 determination is being reviewed?

46 Section 102(3) of the Act makes clear that, where the Tribunal is reviewing a section 86 determination, a range of parties must be allowed to make representation and lead or produce evidence. These are:

- the patient;
- the patient's named person;
- any guardian of the patient;
- any welfare attorney of the patient;
- the patient's MHO;
- the patient's RMO;
- the patient's primary carer;
- any curator *ad litem* appointed in respect of the patient; and
- any other person appearing to the Tribunal to have an interest in the determination. (This could include, for example, the patient's solicitor or a psychologist or other party who is providing care and treatment to the patient.)

What can the Tribunal authorise as a result of reviewing the section 86 determination?

47 In terms of section 102(1) of the Act, the Tribunal can make any of the following decisions where it is reviewing the RMO's section 86 determination to extend the CTO. It can:

- confirm the section 86 determination to extend the order;
- confirm the section 86 determination to extend the order and vary any of the compulsory measures or recorded matters it specifies;
- revoke the section 86 determination to extend the order (this does not necessarily mean that the order would be revoked as its expiry date could be some time after the Tribunal has reviewed the section 86 determination); or
- revoke the section 86 determination and the order itself.

48 The Tribunal must record in the CTO any modifications which it has made to the CTO as a result of any such review.

chapter five

SECTION 86 DETERMINATION TO EXTEND A CTO WITH NO VARIATION OF ITS TERMS (AFTER A MANDATORY REVIEW)

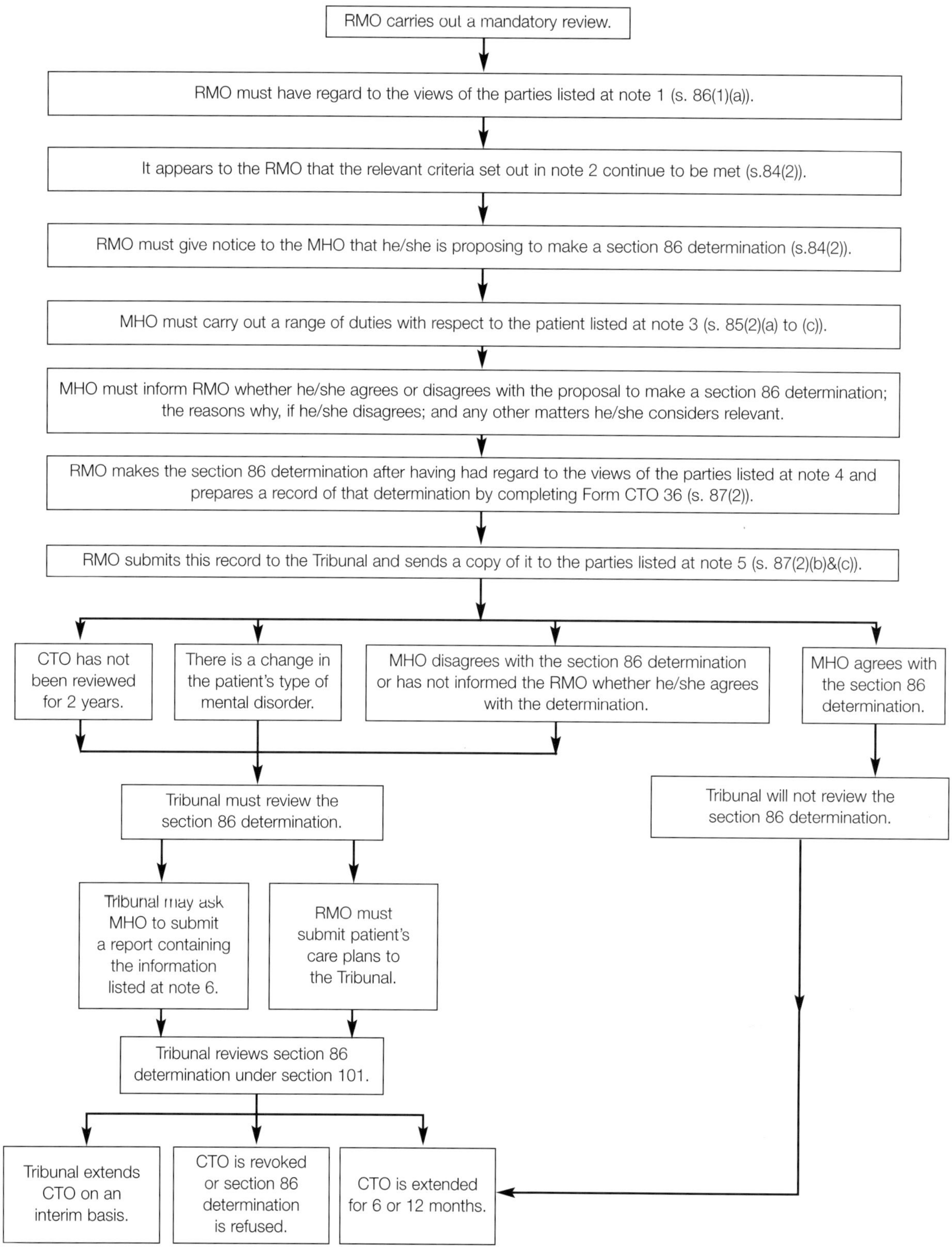

chapter five

Notes on the flowchart explaining the process of making a section 86 determination **(see page 136)**

Note 1: The parties are:

- the patient's MHO;
- any person who provides medical treatment, community care services or other relevant services to the patient as set out in the care plan, in as far as this is seen as appropriate by the RMO;
- any other persons as the RMO considers appropriate.

Note 2: The relevant criteria are that:

- it will continue to be necessary for the patient to be subject to the CTO after the day on which the order is due to expire;
- it is not necessary to vary the compulsory measures or recorded matters specified in the CTO.

Note 3: The MHO must:

- interview the patient, where this is practicable;
- inform the patient of the RMO's proposal to make a section 86 determination;
- inform the patient of his/her rights with respect to that determination;
- inform the patient of the availability of independent advocacy services and help the patient make use of those services.

Note 4: The parties are:

- the MHO;
- any person who provides medical treatment, community care services or other relevant services to the patient as set out in the care plan, in as far as this is seen as appropriate by the RMO;
- any other persons the RMO considers appropriate.

Note 5: The parties are:

- the patient (except where he/she considers there would be a risk of significant harm to the patient or others if that record were sent to the patient);
- the named person;
- the MHO;
- the Commission.

Note 6: The information to be recorded in the MHO's report is:

- the steps taken by the MHO in pursuance of the requirements of MHO's duties to the patient under section 85(2);
- the views of the MHO on the determination and reasons for these;
- if known to the MHO, the patient's views and those of the patient's named person, and reason for those views;
- relevant details of the patient's personal circumstances;
- if known, details of any advance statement made by the patient (and not withdrawn),
- any other information the MHO deems of assistance to the Tribunal in considering the determination.

Extending the CTO with a variation of its terms subsequent to a mandatory review: "A section 92 application"

49 Where the RMO has complied with all the relevant duties connected with the process of carrying out a mandatory review (see paragraphs 7 to 11 above), the RMO may decide that the CTO needs to be extended and that the compulsory measures or recorded matters specified in the order do need to be varied. The processes involved in extending and varying a CTO are more complex than the process for extending the order with no variation of its terms by way of a section 86 determination. This is because the RMO must make a formal application to the Tribunal under section 92 of the Act to seek an extension and variation of the order's terms. The Tribunal must therefore always review the RMO's wish to extend and vary the CTO. The flowchart and notes on pages 146 to 148 illustrate the processes involved in making a section 92 application.

When does an application need to be made? When does an order need to be varied?

50 There are two sets of circumstances under which an application would need to be made to extend and vary the patient's CTO. The first is where one or more of the 8 compulsory measures listed at section 66(1) of the Act is to be added to or deleted from the order. For example, the Tribunal could make a CTO which specifies only 2 compulsory measures: first, the detention of the patient in hospital by way of section 66(1)(a); and, second, the giving of medical treatment by way of section 66(1)(b). On carrying out a mandatory review, the patient's RMO may well be satisfied that although the patient still requires to be subject to compulsory powers, he/she no longer requires to be detained in hospital and the order should instead specify community-based measures (for example, the imposition on the patient of the requirement by way of section 66(1)(d) to attend for medical treatment on specified or directed dates). To remove the hospital detention requirement from the patient's CTO and to add the "attendance requirement", the RMO would have to make an application under section 92 to extend and vary the order.

51 The second set of circumstances under which an application would need to be made to the Tribunal to extend and vary a patient's CTO will depend on what the Tribunal specified in the order. Taking the example of a CTO which imposes a requirement that the patient must attend for medical treatment on specified or directed times, the Tribunal has the choice to specify in the order the times at which the patient must attend for treatment or it can leave such details to the directions of the RMO, see Chapter 3 of this Volume. Where the Tribunal has specified that the patient must attend for treatment, for example, every second Tuesday or twice a week, an application would have to be made to the Tribunal under section 92 to vary those details where the RMO wishes the patient to attend on different dates or at different intervals and where the RMO wishes to extend the order. Where the Tribunal has not specified such detail in the order and has left such detail to the direction of the RMO, no such application would need to be made and the RMO could simply make a determination to extend the CTO under section 86 of the Act.

The RMO must notify the MHO of the proposal to make a section 92 application (section 88(3))

52 Before the RMO can make a section 92 application to the Tribunal, he/she must give notice to the patient's MHO of his/her intention to do so, Specifically, the RMO must notify the MHO of the details of the proposed variation to the order.

53 It would be best practice for the RMO to issue this notification well in advance of the expiry date of the CTO given that the MHO must comply with a range of duties before the application to the Tribunal can be made. It is therefore advisable that the RMO ensures that the MHO has received this notification at least 2 weeks before the CTO is due to expire.

What must the MHO do in advance of the section 92 application being made? (section 89)

54 Upon receiving notification from the RMO that he/she is proposing to make a section 92 application, the MHO must comply with a range of duties which are set out in section 89 of the Act. These are:

- to interview the patient, except where it is impracticable to do so;

- to inform the patient that the RMO is proposing to apply to the Tribunal for an order which would extend the CTO and vary the measures or recorded matters specified in it. The MHO must also inform the patient of the variations which are being proposed as well as of his/her rights in relation to the application;
- to inform the patient of the availability of independent advocacy services and take the appropriate steps to ensure that the patient has the opportunity of making use of those services;
- to inform the RMO whether he/she agrees or disagrees with the proposed application as well as his/her reasons for disagreeing, if that is the case; and
- to inform the RMO of any other matters which he/she considers to be relevant to the application.

55 The principal duty of the MHO in this regard is to evaluate the effectiveness of the care plan, as delivered thus far, and to evaluate the extent to which the objectives of the care plan are being met. The MHO will also need to assess the likely continuing effectiveness of the order if it is extended without any variation of its terms. As with the MHO's duties with respect to a section 86 determination, it would be expected that the MHO would devote as much time and effort to carrying out these duties as he/she would when carrying out similar duties during the CTO application process. *(For further information and best practice guidance on these duties, see Chapter 5 of this Volume of the Code of Practice.)*

56 At section 92(a)(v), the Act raises the possibility of the MHO not complying with the duty to inform the RMO of his/her opinion. However, there are in reality very few conceivable situations in which an MHO should not be able to comply with this duty. If, for reasons of practicability, the patient's designated MHO is unable to comply with the duty within the prescribed timescales, the relevant local authority's MHO service should ensure that an alternative MHO provides the required assessment.

Whom must the RMO notify that the application is going to be made?

57 The patient's RMO is not only under a duty to notify the MHO, as described above, but also to notify the following parties in terms of section 91 of the Act that he/she intends to make a section 92 application. The parties are:

- the patient;
- the patient's named person;
- any guardian of the patient;
- any welfare attorney of the patient;
- the patient's MHO; and
- the Commission.

58 These parties must be given this notification of the application as soon is practicable after the duty to make the application arises. At the very least, this notification must be given before the application to the Tribunal is made. It would be best practice for the RMO to inform the parties representing the patient of his/her intention to make the application verbally, where possible and practicable. Otherwise, the patient or the patient's representatives will have to wait several days before receiving formal written notification of the application. The RMO should also ensure that all the members of the multi-disciplinary team providing care and treatment to the patient have been informed of his/her intention to make the section 92 application.

The RMO must make "a section 92 application" to the Tribunal

59 The RMO can only make the section 92 application to the Tribunal when he/she has complied with the following duties:

- he/she has had regard to the views of the patient's MHO with regard to the proposed application;
- he/she has had regard to the views of any other persons involved in providing treatment, care or other services to the patient with regard to the proposed application;
- he/she is satisfied that it continues to be necessary for the patient to be subject to the CTO but that the order should be varied; and
- he/she has notified various parties of the intention to make the application in terms of section 91 of the Act. These parties are listed at paragraph 57 above.

60 The RMO must make this application as soon as practicable after the need to make the application arises. Any unnecessary delay in making the application could prevent the patient from receiving the care and treatment they require. It is recommended that form CTO4 be used for the purpose of this application.

61 An application made under section 92 of the Act must state the following:
- the patient's name and address;
- the named person's name and address;
- what form of modification of the compulsory measures or any recorded matter(s) is being sought, and the reasons for seeking this modification; and
- whether the patient's MHO agrees or disagrees with the RMO's application to extend and vary the order along with the reasons for the MHO's view. The RMO may alternatively state that the MHO has failed to comply with the duty to inform the RMO of his/her opinion.

Does the Tribunal require any other documents where it is reviewing a section 92 application?

Care Plan

62 Yes. **The Mental Health (Compulsory Treatment Orders – Documents and Reports to be submitted to the Tribunal (Scotland) Regulations 2005 (SSI No. 366)** ("the regulations") provide that the following documents must be provided by the patient's RMO to the Tribunal where it is reviewing a section 92 determination. These are:
- a copy of the patient's care plan first made under section 76 of the Act:
- a copy of the most recent version of that care plan amended under section 76(3) or (4)(a) (where a more recent version exists).

63 The RMO should submit to the Tribunal the two versions of the care plan, where a more recent version exists. It is important that both versions are submitted because the review of the section 86 determination is likely to be taking place several months after the section 76 care plan was first drawn up. It could even be taking place close to 2 years later. It is therefore highly possible that the care plan will have been amended in the intervening period to reflect, for example, changes in the patient's condition; periods during which compulsory measures were suspended; etc. Submitting the two versions will allow the Tribunal to see how (or whether) the objectives of the section 76 care plan have evolved over the period that compulsory measures have been in place and to evaluate the extent to which those objectives are being met.

MHO Report

64 If the Tribunal is of the view it has insufficient information to make a decision, the regulations provide that it may require the patient's MHO to prepare and submit a report which should include the following details:

- the steps taken by the MHO complying with the requirement of the MHO's duties to the patient under section 89(1);
- the views of the MHO on the application and reasons for these;
- if known to the MHO the patient's views and those of the patient's named person, and reason for those views;
- relevant details of the patient's personal circumstances;
- if known, details of any advance statement made by the patient (and not withdrawn); and
- any other information the MHO considers to be of assistance to the Tribunal in considering the application.

Who must be allowed the opportunity to make representation to the Tribunal?

65 Where the Tribunal is determining a section 92 application, it must allow a range of parties to make representation and lead or produce evidence. These parties are:

- the patient;
- the patient's named person;
- any guardian of the patient;
- any welfare attorney of the patient;
- the patient's MHO;
- the patient's RMO;
- the patient's primary carer;
- any curator *ad litem* appointed in respect of the patient; and
- any other person appearing to the Tribunal to have an interest in the application. (This could include, for example, the Commission, the patient's solicitor or a psychologist or other party who is providing care and treatment to the patient.)

What can the Tribunal authorise as a result of determining the section 92 application? (sections 103 & 105 to 108)

66 Section 103 of the Act gives the Tribunal the power to make any of the following decisions with respect to the RMO's section 92 application. It can:
- extend the order and vary any of the compulsory measures or recorded matters specified in the order;
- extend the order (i.e. extend it alone but not vary any of the compulsory measures or recorded matters as had been requested in the section 92 application);
- refuse the section 92 application (this does not mean that the order is revoked and its expiry date could be some time after the Tribunal has reviewed the section 86 determination); or
- refuse the section 92 application and revoke the CTO.

67 If the Tribunal considers that it will not be able to determine the application under section 92 before the CTO expires, it may also grant an order which would modify the CTO on an interim basis. Any such interim order can:
- extend the CTO;
- extend and vary the compulsory measures and/or recorded matter specified in the CTO; or
- vary the compulsory measures and/or recorded matter specified in the CTO.

68 An interim order may not last for more than 28 days, and the total duration of all the interim orders taken together must not be more than a continuous period of 56 days. The Tribunal may grant an interim order on its own initiative or on the application of any party who has an interest in the proceedings. It may also extend a CTO where it is satisfied that it will not be able to determine the section 92 application before the date on which the CTO is due to expire.

69 The Tribunal must record in the CTO any modifications it has made to the CTO as a result of this hearing.

SECTION 92 APPLICATION TO EXTEND A CTO WITH A VARIATION OF ITS TERMS (AFTER A MANDATORY REVIEW)

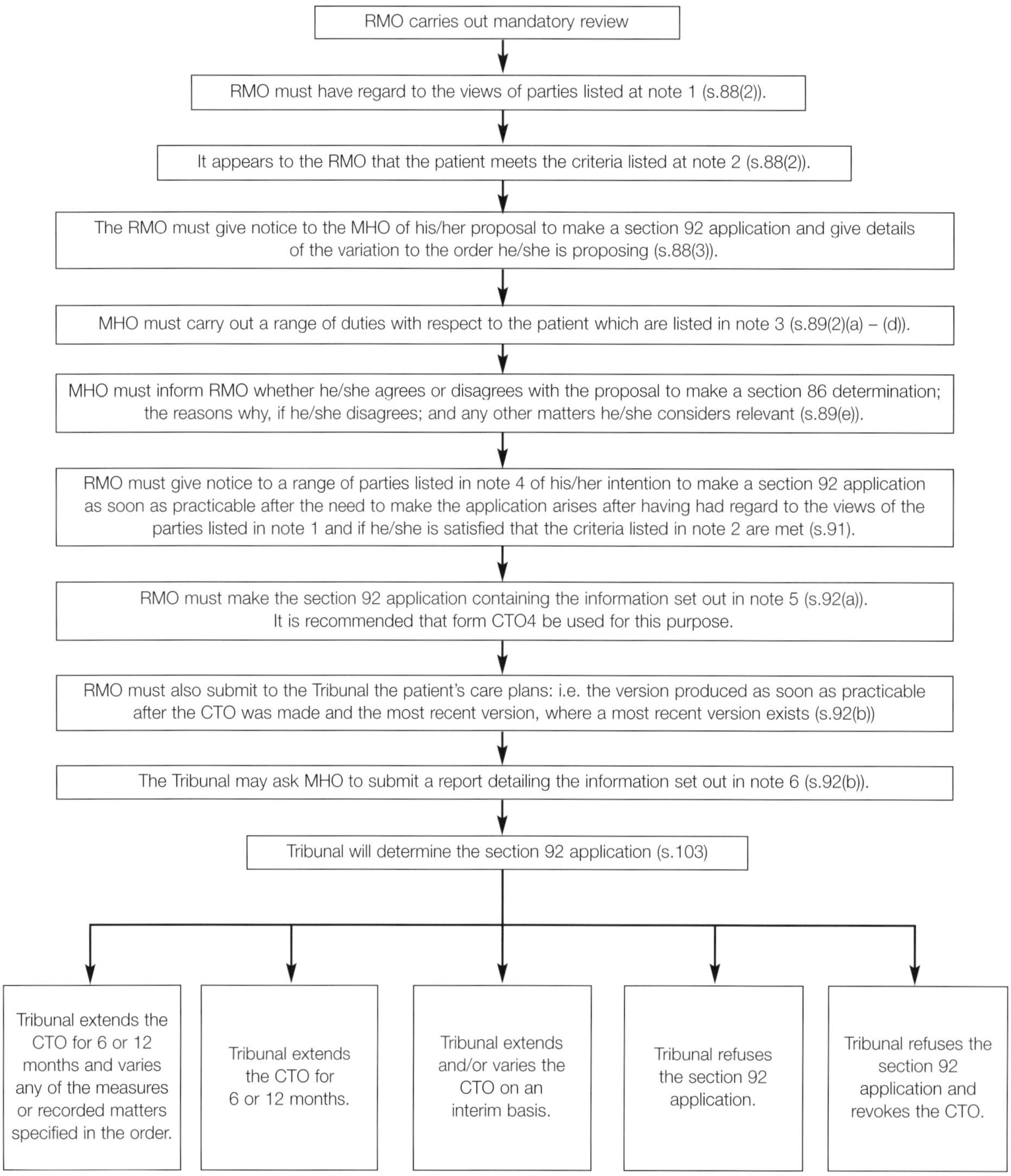

chapter five

Notes on flowchart explaining the process of making a section 92 application

Note 1: The parties are:
- the patient's MHO;
- any person who provides medical treatment, community care services or other relevant services to the patient as set out in the care plan, in as far as this is seen as appropriate by the RMO;
- any other persons the RMO considers appropriate.

Note 2: The criteria are:
- that it will continue to be necessary for the patient to be subject to a CTO after the day on which the order will cease to authorise the measures specified in it;
- that the CTO should be varied by modifying the measures or any recorded matter specified in it.

Note 3: These duties are:
- to interview the patient, where it is practicable to do so;
- to inform the patient of the RMO's proposal to make a section 92 application;
- to inform the patient of the variations to the order which the RMO is proposing and to inform the patient of his/her rights with respect to that determination;
- to inform the patient of the availability of independent advocacy services and help the patient make use of those services.

Note 4: The parties are:
- the patient;
- the patient's named person;
- any guardian and any welfare attorney of the patient;
- the MHO;
- the Commission.

Note 5: The information is:

- the name and address of the patient and of the named person;
- the variation of the terms of the CTO being sought by the RMO and the reasons for seeking that variation;
- whether the MHO agrees/disagrees that the application should be made or whether the MHO has failed to inform the RMO of his/her views.

Note 6: The information to be included is:

- the steps taken by the MHO to comply with the requirement of MHO's duties to the patient under section 89(1);
- the views of the MHO on the application and reasons for these;
- if known to the MHO, the patient's views and those of the patient's named person, and reason for those views;
- relevant details of the patient's personal circumstances;
- if known, details of any advance statement made by the patient (and not withdrawn);
- any other information the MHO considers to be of assistance to the Tribunal in considering the application.

Varying the CTO subsequent to a "from time to time" review: Making "A section 95 application"

70 As a result of a "from time to time" review, rather than a mandatory review, the RMO may decide that the compulsory measures or recorded matters specified in the CTO need to be varied. In such circumstances, an application must be made to the Tribunal under section 95 of the Act. The steps which must be taken throughout this process are set out in sections 93 to 95 of the Act and in the following paragraphs of this Chapter. They are also illustrated by the flowchart on page 154.

When does an application need to be made? When does an order need to be varied?

71 For a discussion of this issue, please see paragraphs 50 and 51 of this chapter.

What must be done before the section 95 application is made?

72 The duties imposed on the RMO in relation to a section 95 application are set out in section 93 of the Act. The RMO must:

- assess the needs of the patient for medical treatment;
- consider which modifications of the compulsory measures or recorded matters specified in the CTO are appropriate; and
- consult the patient's MHO and any other parties whom the RMO considers to be appropriate.

73 If, after having had regard to the views of the MHO and the other relevant parties, the RMO is still satisfied that it would be appropriate for any of the compulsory measures or recorded matters specified in the CTO to be varied, then he/she must make an application to the Tribunal under section 95 for an order which would vary the terms of the CTO. The consultation process leading up to the RMO's decision to make a section 95 application should be as wide and inclusive as is possible under the circumstances and within the bounds of patient confidentiality. Any intention to vary the terms of the CTO should be communicated to the members of the multi-disciplinary care team and to other legitimately interested parties such as carers and relatives, within the bounds of patient confidentiality, and their views sought and taken into account.

Whom must the RMO notify that the application is going to be made?

74 In terms of section 94 of the Act, the parties who must be notified of the RMO's intention to make a section 95 application are:

- the patient;
- the patient's named person;
- any guardian of the patient;
- any welfare attorney of the patient;
- the patient's MHO; and
- the Commission.

75 These parties must be notified *before* the application to the Tribunal is made. Section 94 of the Act makes clear that the RMO must notify these parties as soon as is practicable after the duty to make the application arises. It would be best practice for the RMO to inform the parties representing the patient of his/her intention to make the application verbally, where possible and practicable, rather than oblige the patient or the patient's representatives to wait several days before receiving formal written notification of the application. The RMO should also ensure that all the members of the multi-disciplinary team providing care and treatment to the patient have been informed of his/her intention to make the section 92 application.

How is the section 95 application made?

76 The section 95 application must state the following:

- the patient's name and address;
- the named person's name and address;
- what form of modification of the compulsory measures or any recorded matter(s) is being sought, and the reasons for seeking this modification;
- whether the patient's MHO agrees or disagrees with the RMO's application to vary the CTO and, if he/she disagrees, the reasons for the MHO's view. The RMO may alternatively state that the MHO has failed to comply with the duty to inform the RMO of his/her opinion.

chapter five

Care Plan

77 Yes. **The Mental Health (Compulsory Treatment Orders – Documents and Reports to be submitted to the Tribunal (Scotland) Regulations 2005 (SSI No. 366)** ("the regulations") provide that the following documents must be provided to the Tribunal where it is reviewing a section 95 determination. These are:

- a copy of the patient's care plan first made under section 76 of the Act along with the most recent version of that care plan (where a more recent version exists). This is to be submitted by the patient's RMO.

78 The RMO should submit to the Tribunal the two versions of the care plan, where a more recent version exists. It is important that both versions are submitted because the review of the section 86 determination is likely to be taking place several months after the section 76 care plan was first drawn up. It could even be taking place close to 2 years later. It is therefore highly possible that the care plan will have been amended in the intervening period to reflect, for example, changes in the patient's condition; periods during which compulsory measures were suspended etc.. Submitting the two versions will allow the Tribunal to see how (or whether) the objectives of the section 76 care plan have evolved over the period that compulsory measures have been in place and to evaluate the extent to which those objectives are being met.

79 The RMO should make this application to the Tribunal as soon as is practicable after the need to make the application arises. Any unnecessary delay in making the application could prevent the patient from receiving the care and treatment they require. It is recommended that form CTO5 be used for this purpose of this application.

80 At section 92(a)(v), the Act raises the possibility of the MHO not complying with the duty to inform the RMO of his/her opinion. However, there are in reality very few conceivable situations in which an MHO should not be able to comply with this duty. If, for reasons of practicability, the designated MHO is unable to comply with the duty within the prescribed timescales, the relevant local authority's MHO service should ensure that an alternative MHO provides the required assessment.

Does the Tribunal require any other documents where it is reviewing a section 95 application?

MHO Report

81 If the Tribunal is of the view it has insufficient information to make a decision the regulations provide that it may require the patient's MHO to prepare and submit a report which should include the following details:

- the steps taken by the MHO complying with the requirement of the MHO's duties to the patient under section 89(1);
- the views of the MHO on the application and reasons for these;
- if known to the MHO, the patient's views and those of the patient's named person, and reason for those views;
- relevant details of the patient's personal circumstances;
- if known, details of any advance statement made by the patient (and not withdrawn) and,
- any other information the MHO considers to be of assistance to the Tribunal in considering the application.

Who must be allowed the opportunity to make representation to the Tribunal? (section 103(5)&(6))

82 Where the Tribunal is making a decision on the section 95 application, it must allow a range of parties to make representation and lead or produce evidence. These parties are:

- the patient;
- the patient's named person;
- any guardian of the patient;
- any welfare attorney of the patient;
- the patient's MHO;
- the patient's RMO;
- the patient's primary carer;
- any curator *ad litem* appointed in respect of the patient; and
- any other person appearing to the Tribunal to have an interest in the application. (This could include, for example, the Commission, the patient's solicitor or a psychologist or other party who is providing care and treatment to the patient.)

What can the Tribunal authorise as a result of determining the section 95 application? (sections 103 & 106 to 108)

83 Section 103(4) of the Act gives the Tribunal the power to make any of the following decisions with respect to the RMO's section 95 application. It can:

- vary the CTO by modifying any of the compulsory measures or recorded matters specified in the order;
- refuse the section 95 application to vary the CTO (this does not mean that the order is revoked and its expiry date could be some time after the Tribunal has reviewed the section 86 determination); or
- refuse the section 95 application and revoke the CTO.

84 It should be noted that the Tribunal may grant an interim order varying the compulsory measures or recorded matters specified in the CTO if it feels it is appropriate to do so while it is determining the section 95 application. It may grant an interim order on the application of any party with an interest in the proceedings or on its own initiative. Each interim order varying the CTO can last up to a maximum of 28 days although all the interim orders taken together must note exceed a period of more than 56 days (see section 107 of the Act).

85 The Tribunal must record in the CTO any modifications it has made to the CTO as a result of determining the section 95 applications.

chapter five

Section 95 application to vary a CTO subsequent to a "from time to time" review.

RMO carries out a "from time to time" review.

RMO must assess the needs for medical treatment and consider whether any of the measures or recorded matters specified in the order should be varied (s.93)(a)&(b).

RMO must consult the MHO and any other persons as RMO considers appropriate.

[MHO must carry out a range of duties with respect to the patient and the RMO which are listed in notes 1 and 2 (to be added by section 330 order)].

RMO must give notice to a range of parties listed in notes 3 of his/her intention to make a section 95 application as soon as practicable after the need to make the application arises (s.94).

RMO must make the section 95 application containing the information set out in note 4 (s.95(a)). It is recommended that form CTO5 be used for this purpose.

RMO must also submit to the Tribunal the patient's care plans: the version produced as soon as practicable after the CTO was made and the most recent version, where a more recent version exists (s.95(b)).

The Tribunal may ask MHO to submit a report detailing the information set out in note 5 (s.95(b).

Tribunal will determine the section 95 application (s.103).

- Tribunal extends the CTO for 6 or 12 months and varies any of the measures or recorded matters specified in order.
- Tribunal extends the CTO for 6 or 12 months.
- Tribunal extends and/or varies the CTO on an interim basis.
- Tribunal refuses the section 95 application.
- Tribunal refuses the section 95 application and revokes the CTO.

Notes on the flowchart explaining how to make a section 95 application

Note 1: The duties which the RMO must carry out are to notify the MHO:
- that he/she is proposing to make an application to the Tribunal under s95 of the Act for an order under s103 varying the CTO; and
- of the modification of the measures or any recorded matters, specified in that order which he/she is proposing.

Note 2: The duties which the MHO must carry out are to:
- interview the patient (where practical);
- inform the patient that the RMO is proposing to make an application to the Tribunal varying the compulsion treatment order by modifying the measures or recorded matters specified in it;
- inform the patient of their rights in relation to that application;
- inform the patient of their rights to independent advocacy under s259 of the Act and take appropriate steps to ensure the patient can access those services;
- inform the patient's RMO of whether they agree or disagree with the application being made and their reasons for any disagreement and any other matters that the MHO considers relevant.

Note 3: The parties are:
- the patient;
- the patient's named person;
- any guardian and any welfare attorney of the patient;
- the MHO;
- the Commission.

Note 4: The information is:
- the name and address of the patient and of the named person;
- the variation of the terms of the CTO being sought by the RMO and the reasons for seeking that variation;
- whether the MHO agrees/disagrees that the application should be made or whether the MHO has failed to inform the RMO of his/her views.

Note 5: The information to be included in the MHO's report is:

- the steps taken by the MHO complying with the requirement of MHO's duty to patients;
- the views of the MHO on the application and reasons for these;
- if known to the MHO, the patient's views and those of the patient's named person, and reason for those views;
- relevant details of the patient's personal circumstances;
- if known, details of any advance statement made by the patient (and not withdrawn);
- any other information the MHO deems of assistance to the Tribunal in considering the application.

What other applications can be made to the Tribunal with respect to a CTO?

86 The Act confers powers, rights and duties on several parties to make a range of further applications to the Tribunal. These are:

- the RMO's duty to make a reference to the Tribunal where a recorded matter is not being provided (sections 96 and 97);
- the Commission's power to make a reference to the Tribunal (section 98); and
- the patient's or the named person's right to apply to the Tribunal to revoke a section 86 determination to extend an order (section 99) or to have a CTO revoked or varied (section 100).

87 These applications are dealt with in the remaining paragraphs of this chapter.

The RMO's duty to make a reference to the Tribunal where a recorded matter is not being provided (sections 96, 97 and 104)

88 If the patient's RMO is satisfied that a recorded matter is not being provided, he/she must make a reference to the Tribunal. Before doing so, he/she must consult the patient's MHO and any other relevant parties to find out why this recorded matter is not being provided. After having had regard to any views expressed by the MHO and the other relevant parties, the RMO *must* make a reference to the Tribunal. It would be expected that the RMO make this reference as soon as is practicable after the need to do so arises, and it is recommended that form CTO10 be used for this purpose.

89 The RMO's reference must contain:

- the name and address of the patient;
- the name and address of the patient's named person; and
- the reason for making the reference.

What other documents must be submitted along with the reference?

90 The regulations provide that documents which must be submitted with the reference are:

- a copy of the patient's care plan first made under section 76 of the Act; and
- a copy of the most recent version of that care plan amended under section 76(3) or (4)(a) (where a more recent version exists).

91 The RMO should submit to the Tribunal the two versions of the care plan, where a more recent version exists. It is important that both versions are submitted because the review of the section 86 determination is likely to be taking place several months after the section 76 care plan was first drawn up. It could even be taking place close to 2 years later. It is therefore highly possible that the care plan will have been amended in the intervening period to reflect, for example, changes in the patient's condition; periods during which compulsory measures were suspended; etc. Submitting the two versions will allow the Tribunal to see how (or whether) the objectives of the section 76 care plan have evolved over the period that compulsory measures have been in place and to evaluate the extent to which those objectives are being met.

92 The regulations also provide that where the Tribunal considers that it has insufficient information to enable it to make a decision it may require the MHO to submit a report recording:

- the MHO's views on why the recorded matter is not being provided; and
- any other information which the MHO considers may assist the Tribunal's consideration of the reference made under section 96.

Whom must the RMO notify that a reference has been made? (section 97)

93 Where the RMO makes a reference to the Tribunal, he/she must also give notice of the reference to the following parties in terms of section 97 of the Act:

- the patient;
- the patient's named person;
- any guardian of the patient;
- any welfare attorney of the patient;
- the patient's MHO; and
- the Commission.

94 This notification must be provided as soon as practicable after the duty to make the reference to the Tribunal arises. In practice, this means that the RMO should provide the notification before the reference is submitted to the Tribunal, not after. It would also be expected that the RMO inform the other members of the multi-disciplinary team providing care and treatment to the patient of the fact that a reference has been made.

chapter five

Which parties must be given the opportunity to make representation to the Tribunal?

95 The following parties must be allowed the opportunity to make representation and lead or produce evidence to the Tribunal with respect to any such reference:

- the patient;
- the patient's named person;
- any guardian of the patient;
- any welfare attorney of the patient;
- the patient's MHO;
- the patient's RMO;
- the patient's primary carer;
- any curator *ad litem* appointed in respect of the patient; and
- any other person appearing to the Tribunal to have an interest in the reference (for example, the Commission, the patient's solicitor or a psychologist or other party who is providing care and treatment to the patient.)

What can the Tribunal authorise with respect to this reference? (section 104 & 106 to 108)

96 On receiving a reference from the RMO, the Tribunal can in terms of section 104(1) of the Act make an order which would vary any of the compulsory measures or any recorded matter specified in the order; or revoke the CTO outright.

97 It should be noted that the Tribunal may also grant an order which would vary the compulsory measures or recorded matters specified in the CTO *on an interim basis,* if it feels it is appropriate to do so, while it is determining the reference (see section 106(2) of the Act). It may grant an interim order on the application of any party with an interest in the proceedings or on its own initiative. Each interim order can last up to a maximum of 28 days although all the interim orders taken together must not exceed a period of more than 56 days (see section 107 of the Act).

chapter five

The Commission's power to make a reference to the Tribunal (section 98)

98 The Commission has the power to make a reference to the Tribunal in relation to any aspect of the operation of a CTO. It may do so at any time where it appears appropriate to it to do so. Where the Commission makes such a reference to the Tribunal, it must in terms of section 98(3) provide notification to the following parties:

- the patient;
- the patient's named person;
- any guardian of the patient;
- any welfare attorney of the patient;
- the patient's RMO; and
- the patient's MHO.

99 This will enable these parties to make any necessary investigations into the patient's care and treatment which may be required before they can make representation to the Tribunal. It would also be expected that the RMO would inform the other members of the multi-disciplinary team providing care and treatment to the patient, of the fact that a reference has been made.

100 A reference made to the Tribunal by the Commission must state:

- the name and address of the patient;
- the name and address of the patient's named person; and
- the reason for making the reference.

chapter five

Who must be given the opportunity to make representation to the Tribunal where a reference is made?

101 In terms of section 104(2) and (3) of the Act, the following parties must be allowed the opportunity to make representation and lead or produce evidence to the Tribunal where the Commission makes a reference to the Tribunal:

- the patient;
- the patient's named person;
- any guardian of the patient;
- any welfare attorney of the patient;
- the patient's MHO;
- the patient's RMO;
- the patient's primary carer;
- any curator *ad litem* appointed in respect of the patient; and
- any other person appearing to the Tribunal to have an interest in the reference. (This could include, for example, the patient's solicitor or a psychologist or other party, who is providing care and treatment to the patient.)

What are the powers of the Tribunal with respect to such a reference?

102 Subsequent to such a reference, the Tribunal has the power in terms of section 104(1) of the Act to make an order which would vary any of the compulsory measures or recorded matters specified in the order or which would revoke the CTO.

103 The Tribunal may also grant an order varying the terms of the CTO *on an interim basis,* if it feels it is appropriate to do so, while it is determining the reference (see section 106 of the Act). It may grant an interim order on the application of any party with an interest in the proceedings or on its own initiative. Each interim order can last up to a maximum of 28 days although all the interim orders taken together must not exceed a period of more than 56 days (see section 107 of the Act).

chapter five

The patient's or the named person's right to apply to the Tribunal (sections 99 and 100)

104 There are two applications which the patient or the patient's named person can make to the Tribunal. They are:

- an application under section 99 of the Act to revoke a section 86 determination to extend a CTO; and
- an application under section 100 of the Act to revoke a CTO or to vary any of the compulsory measures or recorded matters specified in the CTO.

When can these applications be made? How many applications can be made? (section 100)

105 With regard to an application made by the patient or by the named person under section 99 to revoke an RMO's section 86 determination to extend a CTO, such an application can be made at any point during the CTO's operation after the point where the RMO has made that section 86 determination.

106 If the Tribunal refuses the application to revoke a section 86 determination, the person who made the application cannot make another application within the 6 month or 12 month period of the CTO continuing in effect. This means that, for example, if a patient's application to revoke a section 86 determination is refused, the patient could not make a second application with respect to that determination. However, even though the patient's application has been refused, the patient's named person could then also apply for a revocation of the determination.

107 With regard to an application by the patient or the named person to revoke or vary a CTO, such an application cannot be made within 3 months of:

- the CTO being made;
- an order which extends the CTO following a section 86 determination; or
- an order which extends the CTO and varies the compulsory measures and/or recorded matters specified in the CTO.

108 Section 100(6) states that the person who made the application (i.e. the patient or the named person) may only make one further application under section 100. This means that the patient and the named person can each make two applications under section 100 within each 6 month or 12 month period of the CTO being in effect.

Who must be afforded the opportunity to make representation to the Tribunal? (section 103(5)&(6))

109 Where the patient or the named person makes such an application to the Tribunal, the following parties must be afforded the opportunity to make representation and lead or produce evidence to the Tribunal:

- the patient;
- the patient's named person;
- any guardian of the patient;
- any welfare attorney of the patient;
- the patient's MHO;
- the patient's RMO;
- the patient's primary carer;
- any curator *ad litem* appointed in respect of the patient; and
- any other person appearing to the Tribunal to have an interest in the reference. (This could include, for example, the Commission, the patient's solicitor or a psychologist or other party who is providing care and treatment to the patient.)

What are the powers of the Tribunal with respect to these applications? (section 103(2) to (4))

110 Where the patient or the named person makes an application to revoke a section 86 determination, the Tribunal has the power to:

- revoke the section 86 determination;
- revoke the section 86 determination and the CTO outright;
- confirm the section 86 determination; or
- confirm the section 86 determination and vary the CTO by modifying any of the compulsory measures or recorded matters specified in it.

111 Where the patient or the named person makes an application to vary or revoke the CTO, the Tribunal has the power to:

- refuse the patient's or named person's application;
- revoke the CTO; or
- vary the CTO by modifying any of the compulsory measures or recorded matters specified in it.

112 It is important to note that in all cases where an appeal is being made to the Tribunal, the presumption is always in favour of revoking the CTO unless the RMO is satisfied that the criteria are met. The onus is not therefore on the patient to demonstrate that he/she no longer meets the criteria.

113 The Tribunal may, in accordance with section 106, grant an interim order which would vary any of the compulsory measures or recorded matters specified in the CTO, if it feels it is appropriate to do so while it is determining the application. The Tribunal may grant an interim order on the application of any party with an interest in the proceedings or on its own initiative. Each interim order can last up to a maximum of 28 days although all the interim orders granted when taken together must not exceed a continuous period of 56 days (see section 107 of the Act).

chapter 6:

non-compliance with a community-based compulsory treatment order or a community-based interim compulsory treatment order

chapter six

Introduction

This chapter examines Part 7 Chapter 5 (sections 112 to 123) of the Act. It sets out the processes to be followed where a patient who is subject to a CTO or an interim CTO does not comply with the compulsory measures specified in the order other than the compulsory measure which authorises the patient's detention in hospital (for example, where a patient does not attend for medical treatment in accordance with the terms of their CTO).

This chapter does not deal with a situation in which a patient "absconds". Part 20 of the Act and Chapter 8 of this Volume of the Code of Practice examine that eventuality.

Overview of non-compliance procedures

01 Part 7 Chapter 5 of the Act deals with the powers and procedures which are relevant to a patient who has not complied with any community-based compulsory measure specified in a CTO or an interim CTO – that is, any compulsory measure other than the requirement which can be imposed on a patient by way of section 66(1)(a) of the Act to be detained in hospital. *For further information on a situation where a patient fails to comply with the requirement to be detained in hospital, see the provisions relating to absconding which can be found in Part 20 of the Act.*

02 Part 7 Chapter 5 of the Act provides for two sets of powers with respect to situations in which a patient does not comply with community-based compulsory measures. The first, described in sections 113 to 115 of the Act, relates to a lack of compliance with any community-based compulsory measure. This set of powers is discussed in paragraphs 4 to 27 of this Chapter and is illustrated by the flowchart on page 176. The second set of powers, described at section 112 of the Act, can be exercised with respect to a lack of compliance with the "attendance requirement" alone. (The attendance requirement is the compulsory measure which can be specified in a CTO or interim CTO by way of section 66(1) (c) of the Act.) These powers are discussed in paragraphs 30 to 33 of this chapter.

Which set of powers should be exercised?

03 It would be expected that, where the only compulsory measure not to have been complied with is the attendance requirement, the powers under section 112 of the Act would be exercised in preference to the powers exercisable under sections 113 to 123 of the Act. This is because they may be more likely to help professionals comply with the principle of treating the patient within an environment which appears to involve the minimum restriction on the freedom of the patient necessary in the circumstances. The final decision as to which set of powers are most appropriate where a patient has not complied with the attendance requirement will, however, ultimately depend on a wide range of factors which might include:

- the individual circumstances of the patient;
- the views of the patient as to what constitutes a lesser restriction on his/her freedom;
- whether the RMO considers that the criteria set out at section 113(2) or 113(3) of the Act are met; and
- whether the RMO considers that a more thorough medical examination of the patient than could be carried out in the 6 hour detention period authorised by section 112(4) of the Act is required with a view to determining whether a section 95 application to vary the terms of the CTO should be made to the Tribunal.

chapter six

Lack of compliance with compulsory measures where hospital detention is not authorised (sections 113 to 123)

04 Where a patient fails to comply with any community-based compulsory measure specified in a CTO or an interim CTO, the RMO can exercise two powers under section 113(4) and (5) of the Act:

- the power to take the patient or to have the person taken into custody and conveyed to a hospital; and
- the power to detain the patient in hospital for a period of 72 hours beginning with the patient's arrival in hospital.

05 The Act does not specify the length of time a person may be held in custody under these powers. However, it would always be expected that the patient would be conveyed to hospital immediately and would be held in custody for as short a time as is practicably possible.

06 There are two sets of circumstances in which the patient's RMO can exercise the power to take the patient into custody and convey him/her to hospital. This power can be exercised where:

- reasonable steps have been taken to contact the patient following his/her lack of compliance with the compulsory measure;
- the patient has been afforded a reasonable opportunity to comply with the compulsory measure in a case where contact has been made with the patient; and
- it is reasonably likely that there would be a significant deterioration in the patient's mental health if the patient were to continue to fail to comply with the compulsory measure.

07 The second set of circumstances is set out at section 113(3) of the Act and is likely to be most relevant to a patient who is subject to a community-based CTO but whose mental health has deteriorated suddenly and significantly. The circumstances are where:

- it is reasonably likely that there would be a significant deterioration in the patient's mental health if the patient were to continue to fail to comply with the compulsory measure; and
- it is necessary as a matter of urgency to exercise the power to take the patient or have the patient taken into custody in terms of section 113(4) of the Act.

08 In judging whether reasonable steps have been taken to contact the patient following any non-compliance with a compulsory measure, in line with section 113(2)(a) of the Act, it would be best practice for the RMO to ensure that as extensive enquiries as practicable have been made with the patient and with the patient's named person, independent advocate, carers or relatives, community care providers, etc, as to why the compulsory measure has not been complied with. Similarly, as much information as practicable regarding the patient's current mental health and the circumstances surrounding the lack of compliance with the compulsory measure should be solicited from other members of the patient's multi-disciplinary team, particularly the patient's MHO and any person providing care and treatment to the patient in the community.

09 It is important, however, that such information sharing is seen as a two-way process. In other words, even though the final decision with respect to what to do about the patient's lack of compliance with the compulsory measure must be made by the RMO, all the relevant members of the multi-disciplinary team should be pro-active in helping the RMO establish the facts surrounding the patient's circumstances and non-compliance with the compulsory measure.

10 The RMO must also, in terms of section 113(2)(b) of the Act, consider whether the patient has been afforded a reasonable opportunity to comply with the compulsory measure before exercising any power to detain the patient in hospital. It would be expected that the decision to detain the patient in hospital would be seen as a last resort. It would also be expected that such a decision would only be taken once the relevant members of the patient's multi-disciplinary team have exhausted all the appropriate and practicable means of gaining the patient's compliance with the relevant compulsory measure.

11 If the RMO considers that reasonable steps have been taken to contact the patient and to afford the patient the opportunity to comply with the measure, he/she may exercise his/her powers under section 113(4) of the Act to take the patient or have the patient taken into custody and conveyed to hospital. In any case where the patient is being taken into custody, the process should be handled with sensitivity and flexibility. It would be good practice to ensure that the roles and responsibilities of all the parties who might potentially be involved in taking the patient into custody, including the police, are carefully defined in line with those laid

out in locally developed and agreed on Psychiatric Emergency Plans. It will be particularly important to ensure police involvement within the development of such plans, particularly with respect to putting in place robust risk assessment procedures. *(For further information on Psychiatric Emergency Plans, see Chapter 7 of this Volume of the Code of Practice.)*

12 The use of police cells while the patient is being held in custody should be avoided in all but the most exceptional circumstances.

13 Where the patient has been conveyed to hospital in such circumstances, the RMO also has the power under section 113(5) of the Act to detain the patient for a period of 72 hours beginning with the time of the patient's arrival at the hospital. The patient should only be detained in such circumstances where he/she does not or cannot consent to remaining in hospital on a voluntary basis.

14 As soon as reasonably practicable after the patient has been conveyed to the hospital, the patient's RMO must carry out a medical examination of the patient. In terms of section 113(6)(b) of the Act, the RMO may alternatively make arrangements for another approved medical practitioner to carry out such a medical examination. It would, however, always be best practice for the patient's RMO to carry out this medical examination.

Further period of hospital detention following lack of compliance with compulsory measures

15 Sections 114 and 115 of the Act confer on the patient's RMO further powers where a patient has not complied with the terms of a community-based CTO or interim CTO and has been detained in hospital for a period of 72 hours under the terms of section 113(5) of the Act. Section 114 relates to a patient subject to a CTO while section 115 relates to a patient subject to an interim CTO.

16 Where a patient is subject to a CTO when the failure to comply with the compulsory measure occurs, the patient's RMO may grant a certificate which would detain him/her in hospital for a further period of 28 days where certain criteria apply. These criteria are:

- the patient is currently detained in hospital under section 113(5) of the Act (i.e. detained for up to 72 hours after being taken into custody and conveyed to hospital under section 113(4));
- the patient has been examined by either his/her RMO or another approved medical practitioner in terms of section 113(6) of the Act;
- the RMO is considering whether the compulsory measures currently specified in the CTO need to be modified or is satisfied that an application under section 95 of the Act needs to be made to the Tribunal to vary the compulsory measures specified in the CTO;
- the RMO considers that it is reasonably likely that there will be a significant deterioration in the patient's mental health if the patient does not continue to be detained in hospital;
- the RMO has consulted and obtained the consent of the patient's MHO to the proposed continued detention; and
- the RMO has consulted the patient's named person, where this was practicable to do so.

17 Where all these criteria have been met, the RMO may grant a certificate under section 114(2) of the Act authorising the patient's continued detention in hospital for a period of 28 days. This 28 day period begins at the point when the certificate was granted. In terms of section 114(5) of the Act, this certificate must be signed by the RMO and must state his/her reasons for believing that it is reasonably likely that there will be a significant deterioration in the patient's mental health if the patient does not continue to be detained in hospital.

18 Where a patient is subject to an interim CTO when the failure to comply with a compulsory measure occurred, the patient's RMO may grant a certificate under section 115(2) of the Act authorising the patient's continued detention in hospital from the point of the certificate being granted to the point of the interim CTO expiring. Such a certificate could only be granted where certain limited criteria apply. These criteria are:

- the patient is currently detained in hospital under section 113(5) of the Act (i.e. detained for 72 hours after being taken into custody and conveyed to hospital under section 113(4));
- the patient has been examined by either his/her RMO or another approved medical practitioner in terms of section 113(6) of the Act;
- the RMO considers that it is reasonably likely that there will be a significant deterioration in the patient's mental health if the patient does not continue to be detained in hospital;
- the interim CTO will not have expired by the time the 72 hour detention period authorised by section 113(5) of the Act expires;
- the RMO has consulted and obtained the consent of the patient's MHO; and
- the RMO has consulted the patient's named person, where this was practicable to do so.

19 Where all these criteria have been met, the RMO may grant a certificate under section 115(2) of the Act authorising the patient's continued detention in hospital until the expiry of the interim CTO. This certificate must be signed by the RMO and must state his/her reasons for believing that it is reasonably likely that there will be a significant deterioration in the patient's mental health if the patient does not continue to be detained in hospital.

20 Any certificate issued under sections 114(2) or 115(2) of the Act must be followed up by a series of notifications in terms of section 116 of the Act. The managers of the hospital in which the patient is detained must notify the following parties of the granting of either certificate as soon as practicable after it was granted:

- the patient;
- the patient's named person;
- any guardian of the patient; and
- any welfare attorney of the patient.

21 These hospital managers must also notify the Tribunal and the Commission within 7 days of the certificate being granted. They must also send a copy of the certificate to these parties within the same timescale.

22 The patient's RMO is under a duty by way of sections 117 and 118 of the Act to revoke any certificate issued under sections 114(2) and 115(2) where certain circumstances apply. With respect to a certificate issued under section 114(2) (that is, with respect to a patient who is subject to a CTO), these circumstances are:

- where the patient's RMO is satisfied that the compulsory measures specified in the CTO do not in fact need to be modified; or
- where the patient's RMO is required to make an application to the Tribunal under section 95 of the Act, but is not satisfied that it is reasonably likely that there will be a significant deterioration in the patient's mental health if the patient does not continue to be detained in hospital.

23 With respect to a patient subject to an interim CTO and a certificate issued under section 115(2) of the Act, these circumstances are:

- where the patient's RMO is not satisfied that it is reasonably likely that there will be a significant deterioration in the patient's mental health if the patient does not continue to be detained in hospital.

24 In any case where the patient's RMO considers it appropriate to revoke a certificate issued under sections 114(2) or 115(2) of the Act, it would be best practice for him/her to first discuss the proposed revocation with the patient's MHO and other members of the patient's multi-disciplinary team and the patient's carers, where applicable, to ensure that suitable arrangements continue to be in place for the patient's care and treatment when he/she is no longer in hospital.

25 In any case where the patient's RMO revokes a certificate issued under sections 114(2) or 115(2) of the Act, he/she must provide notification, in terms of section 119, to certain parties as soon as practicable after the revocation. These parties are:

- the patient;
- the patient's named person;
- any guardian of the patient; and
- any welfare attorney of the patient.

26 The RMO must also notify the Tribunal and the Commission of any such revocation within 7 days of the certificate being revoked. It would also be best practice to ensure that the patient's MHO has been notified of any such revocation.

27 Under section 120 of the Act, the patient and the patient's named person both have a right to apply to the Tribunal to revoke any certificate which has been granted under sections 114(2) or 115(2) of the Act. On such an application, the Tribunal must revoke the relevant certificate where it is not satisfied that it is reasonably likely that there will be a significant deterioration in the patient's mental health if the patient does not continue to be detained in hospital.

Interaction between a CTO or an interim CTO and any detention period or certificate authorised under sections 113 to 115

28 Section 121 of the Act describes the interaction between a CTO or an interim CTO and the detention period of 72 hours authorised by section 113(5) of the Act (that is, the 72 hour period of hospital detention subsequent to a patient's non-compliance with any of the compulsory measures specified in a CTO or an interim CTO). During this 72 hour detention period, the compulsory measures specified in the CTO or interim CTO are suspended. The one exception to this relates to the compulsory measure listed at section 66(1) (b) of the Act: that is, the giving of medical treatment to the patient under Part 16 of the Act. This compulsory measure continues to be authorised by the CTO or interim CTO throughout the period of detention authorised by section 113(5) of the Act.

29 Sections 122 and 123 of the Act describe the interaction between a CTO or an interim CTO and the certificates issued under sections 114(2) and 115(2) of the Act (that is, the certificates which could be issued authorising detention subsequent to a 72 hour period of detention under section 113(5)). During the continued detention period authorised by either of these certificates, the compulsory measures specified in the CTO or the interim CTO are suspended. The one exception to this rule is the compulsory measure listed at section 66(1) (b) of the Act: that is, the giving of medical treatment to the patient under Part 16 of the Act. This compulsory measure continues to be authorised by the CTO or interim CTO throughout the period of detention authorised by the section 114(2) or section 115(2) certificate.

Lack of compliance with the "attendance requirement" (section 112)

30 Section 112 of the Act confers certain powers on the patient's RMO in relation to a patient's lack of compliance with an "attendance requirement" specified in a CTO or an interim CTO. An attendance requirement compels a patient to attend specified places at specified times with a view to being given medical treatment for their mental disorder (see section 66(1)(c) of the Act). Where a patient does not comply with an attendance requirement, section 112 of the Act authorises the RMO to take certain steps either in addition to or as an alternative to the powers he/she may exercise under sections 113 to 115 of the Act. The RMO may take or may have the patient taken into custody and conveyed to the place where they were to receive their medical treatment or to any hospital. The patient can be detained at that place or hospital for no more than 6 hours from the point of arrival. The purpose of the 6 hour detention period is to administer the medical treatment in accordance with Part 16 of the Act to the patient which he/she would have been given had he/she complied with the attendance requirement. Medical treatment should not be forcibly administered to the patient in their own home.

31 Before exercising this power, however, the patient's RMO must consult and obtain the consent of an MHO in terms of section 112(2) of the Act. Where practicable, it would be good practice for the RMO to ensure that consent is sought from and granted by the MHO who has been designated under section 229 of the Act as having responsibility for that patient's case.

32 If the CTO or interim CTO does not specify the giving of medical treatment to the patient under Part 16 of the Act, the patient's RMO may use the 6 hour detention period to determine whether the patient is capable of consenting to medical treatment. In accordance with section 112(4)(b) of the Act, where the patient is capable of giving consent, the RMO should determine whether the patient does indeed consent to receive any medical treatment.

33 Where a patient fails to comply with the attendance requirement specified in the CTO or interim CTO, it would be expected that the RMO would take all the steps which are reasonable and practicable under the circumstances to investigate why the patient has been unable to comply with the attendance requirement before exercising the power to take the patient or to have the patient taken into custody. It would therefore be standard practice for the RMO to ensure that the reasonable steps which would be taken before exercising powers under section 113 or 114 would also be taken here before the power to detain the patient for 6 hours is exercised.

chapter six

FLOWCHART ILLUSTRATING THE PROCEDURES TO BE FOLLOWED WHERE A PATIENT SUBJECT TO A COMMUNITY-BASED CTO OR INTERIM CTO DOES NOT COMPLY WITH A COMPULSORY MEASURE AUTHORISED IN THE ORDER

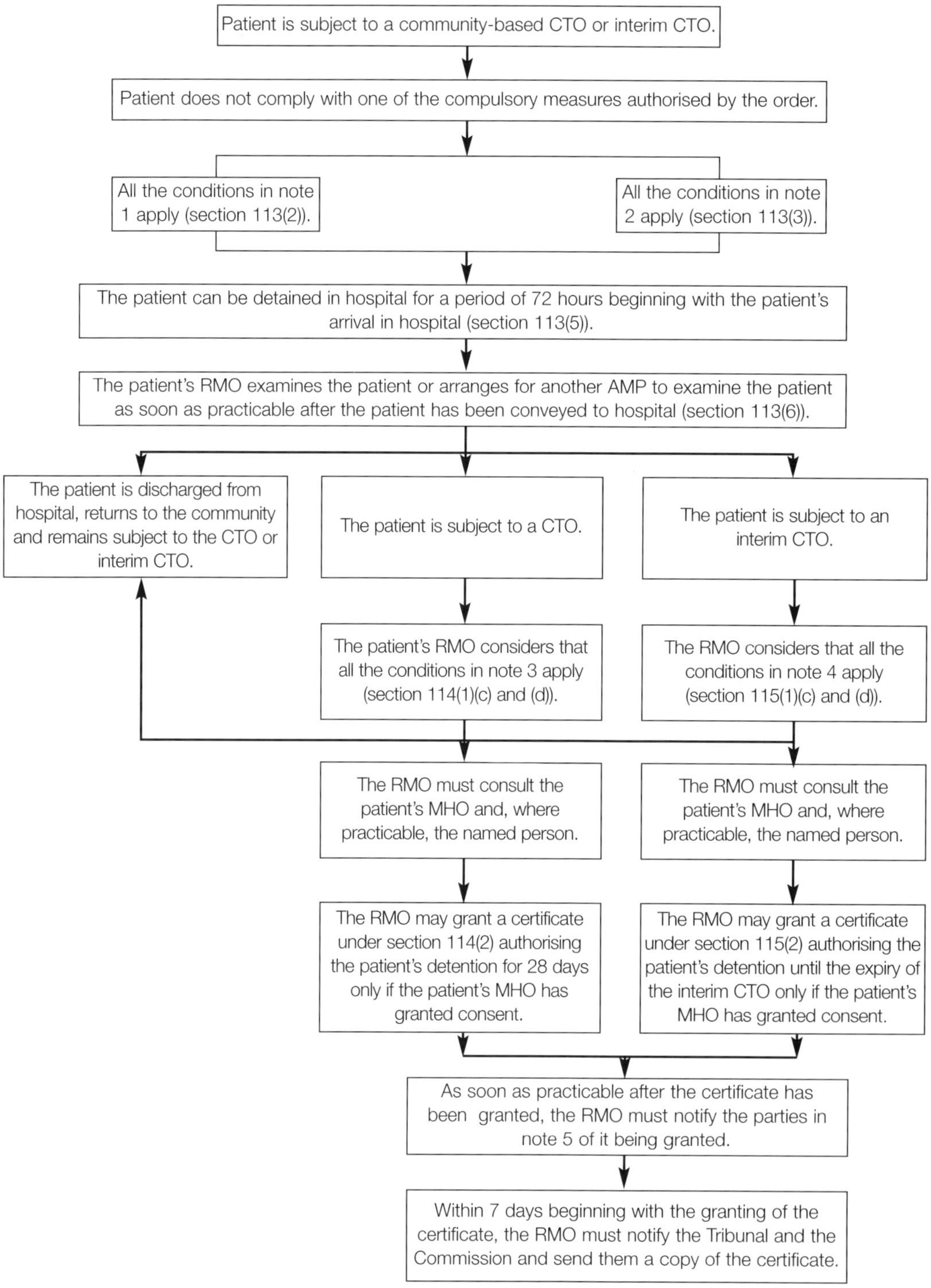

Notes relating to the flowchart illustrating the procedures to be followed where a patient subject to a community-based CTO or interim CTO does not comply with a compulsory measure authorised in the order

Note 1: The RMO considers that:

- reasonable steps have been taken to contact the patient following the patient's non-compliance with a compulsory measure;
- the patient has been afforded a reasonable opportunity to comply with the measure (if contact has been made with the patient);
- it is reasonably likely that there would be a significant deterioration in the patient's mental health if he/she were to continue to fail to comply with the compulsory measure.

Note 2: The RMO considers that:

- it is reasonably likely that there would be a significant deterioration in the patient's mental health if he/she were to continue to fail to comply with the compulsory measure;
- it is necessary as a matter of urgency to take the patient into custody and convey him/her to a hospital.

Note 3: The patient's RMO:

- is considering whether the CTO needs to be varied or has decided that a section 95 does need to be made;
- considers that it is reasonably likely that there would be a significant deterioration in the patient's mental health if he/she does not continue to be detained in hospital.

Note 4: The conditions are:

- the patient's RMO considers that there will be a significant deterioration in the patient's mental health if he/she does not continue to be detained in hospital;
- the interim CTO will not have expired by the time the 72 hour period of detention authorised by section 113(5) expires.

Note 5: The parties are:

- the patient;
- the patient's named person;
- any guardian or welfare attorney of the patient.

chapter 7
emergency detention certificate (part 5)

chapter seven

Introduction

This chapter sets out the procedures which must be followed where the granting of an emergency detention certificate is being considered in accordance with the provisions of Part 5 of the Act.

The chapter begins with a general overview of the provisions which relate to the granting of a certificate as a means of establishing the framework in which emergency detention operates.

The remainder of the chapter traces the specific procedures which must be gone through for a valid emergency detention certificate to be granted.

The chapter closes with a discussion of the processes allied to the granting of a "suspension certificate": that is, a certificate which will temporarily suspend the requirement that the patient be detained in hospital.

Two flowcharts can be found at the end of this chapter. The first which is followed by a set of explanatory notes illustrates the statutory procedures to be followed by a medical practitioner when granting an emergency detention certificate. The second examines the occasions where an incapacity certificate may need to be granted under section 47 of the Adults with Incapacity (Scotland) Act 2000 instead of or in addition to an emergency detention certificate under the Act.

Overview of emergency detention

How long does a period of emergency detention last and when does the detention period begin?

01 The detention period is 72 hours.

02 If a person is not in hospital before the emergency detention certificate is granted, the granting of the certificate authorises two separate procedures. These are:

- their transfer to hospital. This transfer must take place within 72 hours of the certificate being granted; and
- their detention in hospital for a further 72 hours.

03 Please see paragraph 22 of the Introduction Chapter of this Volume for further information with respect to how these time periods should be interpreted.

chapter seven

04 The granting of the emergency detention certificate does not in itself authorise the person's detention in hospital where the patient was in the community before the certificate was granted. Section 36(7) of the Act states that the detention of such a patient is authorised only if the emergency detention certificate has been given to the managers of the hospital in which the person is to be detained before the person is admitted to the hospital under the authority of that certificate. Therefore, with respect to a patient who was in the community prior to the certificate being granted, the 72 hour detention period therefore begins with the patient's admission to hospital under the authority of the certificate. It should be noted that the certificate does not have to be given to the managers of the hospital themselves. It may be given to a party acting on their behalf such as a member of the nursing staff on the admitting ward.

05 If a patient is already a hospital in-patient when an emergency detention certificate is granted, he/she may be detained for a total period of 72 hours. For such a patient the 72 hour period of detention begins at the point when the certificate was granted. Note also that the certificate gives authority to transfer the person from one hospital to another during that 72 hour period.

06 If a patient is in an Accident and Emergency Department and has not yet been admitted to hospital when the emergency detention certificate was granted, the patient should be considered as having been in the community prior to the certificate being granted, and the timescales relevant to a community-based patient should apply.

07 Although the transfer and detention periods have been described in the preceding paragraphs as 72 hours, these time periods should be understood as meaning up to 72 hours. The person should only be detained for as short a time as is possible and appropriate. If it is likely that a period of hospital detention lasting longer than 72 hours may be appropriate, a short-term detention certificate should be granted as early as is practicable and appropriate within the 72 hour period of emergency detention. The emergency detention certificate is revoked automatically on the granting of the short-term detention certificate.

08 It is important to note that a short-term detention certificate should be granted in preference to an emergency detention certificate, where this is practicable and where the relevant criteria have been met. *For further information on this issue, please see paragraphs 20 to 21 of this Chapter as well as the overview of compulsory powers to be found in Chapter 2 of this Volume of the Code of Practice.*

Who may not be made subject to a period of emergency detention?

09 Section 36 of the Act states that an emergency detention certificate may not be issued if, immediately before the medical examination is carried out, the person is detained in hospital by way of any of the following authorities:

- an emergency detention certificate;
- a short-term detention certificate;
- an extension certificate granted under section 47 of the Act;
- section 68 of the Act; and
- a certificate granted under sections 114(2) or 115(2) of the Act.

Who has the authority to grant an emergency detention certificate?

10 Any registered medical practitioner may grant an emergency detention certificate: it is not necessary for the practitioner to be an approved medical practitioner. The practitioner must be a fully registered medical practitioner within the meaning of the Medical Act 1983.

11 An emergency detention certificate may not be granted by a different practitioner from the one who carried out the medical examination.

12 Best practice would suggest that the most suitable medical practitioner to grant the emergency detention certificate is the medical practitioner within the multi-disciplinary team currently responsible for the patient's care, in any case where the patient is already known to mental health services. For an in-patient, this would be the patient's current responsible medical consultant or his/her deputy. For a person who was in the community when the certificate was granted, this is likely to be their general medical practitioner. It would, however, of course be inappropriate in a situation of immediate risk to dispute which medical practitioner should grant the certificate. A pragmatic approach should be adopted in these circumstances, and the first practitioner to come into contact with the patient allowed to grant the certificate.

chapter seven

Conflicts of interest with respect to emergency detention

13 No regulations have been made under section 36(3) of the Act so in effect there can be no conflict of interest.

14 Nevertheless the detaining medical practitioner should bear in mind that it would be best practice to avoid becoming involved in the detention of a colleague, close relation or friend wherever possible. An MHO who believes that a conflict of interest might arise in relation to the proposed detention should request his/her local authority employers to allocate another MHO to deal with the case.

Is there a right of appeal against emergency detention?

15 No, the patient has no formal right of appeal against the granting of an emergency detention certificate. However, the patient's rights are protected by a range of factors which include:

- an MHO must, wherever practicable, be consulted and his/her consent sought to the granting of the emergency detention certificate;
- the medical practitioner who grants the certificate must provide on the certificate a justification of his/her reasons for granting the certificate;
- the managers of the hospital in which the patient is detained must notify the relevant local authority of the reasons why it was impracticable to consult and seek the consent of an MHO to the granting of the certificate, where this was the case;
- the Commission has the power under section 11 of the Act to investigate a case where a patient is subject to emergency detention;
- if it is deemed that ongoing detention would be appropriate, then the emergency detention certificate should be revoked as quickly as is practicable and a short-term detention certificate granted instead;
- the patient may not be given medical treatment in terms of Part 16 of the Act while subject to an emergency detention certificate; and
- the patient has a right of access to independent advocacy services under section 259 of the Act.

Are emergency detention procedures relating to hospital in-patients different from those relating to a person who was in the community when the certificate was granted?

16 No, the statutory procedures with respect to the granting of the certificate are the same. It should be remembered, however, that a hospital in-patient may only be detained on the authority of the emergency detention certificate for a total of 72 hours. The 2-stage process of 72 hours for the patient's removal to hospital followed by a further 72 hours of hospitalisation does not apply where an emergency detention certificate is granted with respect to a hospital in-patient.

17 Where a medical practitioner believes that it may be appropriate to grant an emergency detention certificate with respect to an informal in-patient, he/she would be well advised to discuss with that in-patient the various options for treatment including the possibility as a last resort of formal detention under the Act. The medical practitioner will also wish to ensure that the informal patient is provided with written information regarding their rights (for example, the right to apply to the Tribunal in relation to unlawful detention under section 291 of the Act).

18 Where an informal patient wishes to leave hospital against medical advice, he/she should not be placed in the position of feeling he/she must agree to stay in hospital purely because of the possibility of being detained under the Act. Such 'de facto detention' places restrictions on an informal patient without according him/her the protection of the rights he/she would be accorded were he/she to be formally detained; and it is important to remember that the patient's perception of whether or not he/she is likely to be detained if he/she does not comply with the medical practitioner's wishes is an important factor in deciding whether or not the patient is subject to 'de facto detention'.

19 It would, however, be appropriate for nursing staff to explain to a patient who is considering discharging him/herself or attempting to leave hospital the consequences of doing so: for example, that the nurse's holding power under section 299 of the Act could be exercised with a view to assessing whether the patient meets the criteria for the granting of an emergency or a short-term detention certificate. Nonetheless, an emergency detention certificate should never be granted purely as a means of preventing an informal patient from leaving hospital: the criteria for emergency detention at section 36 of the Act must always be met before the power may be exercised.

Processes preceding the granting of the emergency detention certificate

What are the criteria to be used when deciding whether an emergency detention certificate should be granted?

20 The criteria which must be met are laid out in section 36 of the Act. The medical practitioner must consider it likely that:

- the patient has a mental disorder; and
- because of that mental disorder, the patient's decision-making ability with regard to medical treatment for that mental disorder is significantly impaired.

21 The practitioner must also be satisfied that:

- it is necessary as a matter of urgency to detain the patient in hospital in order to determine what medical treatment should be provided to the patient for the suspected mental disorder;
- there would be a significant risk to the health, safety or welfare of the patient or to the safety of another person if the patient were not detained in hospital; and
- making arrangements with a view to granting a short-term detention certificate would involve undesirable delay.

22 It should be noted that the above conditions are cumulative: that is, that all five conditions must be met before the emergency detention certificate can be granted.

23 In instances where the practitioner believes that the patient will not undergo treatment voluntarily during the detention period even if the patient claims to consent to treatment before or at the beginning of the detention period, the practitioner should use his/her judgement to decide whether the patient's claim can be relied upon. This requires a close examination of the person's previous psychiatric history and also as full and proper a consultation between the medical practitioners, the MHO and relevant other parties providing care and treatment to the patient as patient confidentiality allows.

chapter seven

When should an emergency detention certificate be granted?

24 An emergency detention certificate may be granted where the criteria at section 36 of the Act are met (see paragraphs 20 and 21 above). However, a short-term detention certificate should be granted, wherever possible, in preference to an emergency detention certificate, where this is practicable and where the relevant detention criteria have been met. A short-term detention certificate is the preferred "gateway order" because, as compared with an emergency detention certificate, it can only be granted by an approved medical practitioner; the consent of an MHO to the granting of a short-term detention certificate is mandatory; and it confers on the patient and the patient's named person a more extensive set of rights, including the right to make an application to the Tribunal to revoke the certificate.

25 When any decision about whether or not to grant an emergency or short-term detention certificate is being made, the difference in the criteria for emergency and short-term detention, as set out in sections 36 and 44 of the Act respectively, is paramount. In addition to these criteria, practitioners may also wish to consider other factors before deciding on whether it would be more appropriate to grant an emergency detention certificate or a short-term detention certificate. These could include:

- whether urgent action must be taken, and whether there is, as a result of this urgency, insufficient time to comply with the more extensive procedures allied to the granting of a short-term detention certificate;
- whether the medical practitioner is satisfied that the assessment for treatment could not be made with the patient's consent; and
- whether an approved medical practitioner or an MHO is immediately or directly available to grant or consent to the granting of a short-term detention certificate.

26 Where the clinical urgency of the situation will not permit the granting of a short-term detention certificate, it should be borne in mind that the primary purpose of an emergency detention certificate is to permit a full assessment of a person's mental state. It is not to administer medical treatment for the suspected mental disorder. Such treatment may, however, be given where it is urgently required under the authority of section 243 of the Act.

Emergency detention and the Adults with Incapacity (Scotland) Act 2000

27 A medical practitioner will need to decide whether a patient's condition and circumstances necessitate detention under the authority of an emergency detention certificate granted under this Act and/or whether the patient requires to be treated under the authority of a section 47 certificate granted under the Adults with Incapacity (Scotland) Act 2000 ("the 2000 Act"). This decision will depend on the nature of the intervention required and whether the patient meets the relevant criteria under the 2000 Act: for example, in relation to his/her capacity. An emergency detention certificate granted under this Act only provides a power to hold the person in hospital with no authority to provide medical treatment for mental or physical disorder. Where medical treatment for the mental disorder is *urgently* required, however, interventions are authorised under section 243 of the 2003 Act.

28 A certificate under section 47 of the 2000 Act, on the other hand, permits medical treatment for a physical disorder or for mental disorder where the patient is incapable in terms of section 1(6) of that Act of reaching a decision as to medical treatment. A section 47 certificate does not authorise the use of force or detention unless it is immediately necessary and only for as long as necessary in the circumstances. Moreover, it does not allow for a patient's detention in hospital for the purpose of being given medical treatment for mental disorder against his/her will. Detention with respect to treatment for mental disorder should be dealt with under mental health legislation. Where the patient is assessed as requiring medical treatment for a mental disorder but the patient objects and/or requires to be detained to administer that treatment, medical staff should have recourse to procedures under the 2003 Act rather than the 2000 Act.

29 There may additionally be occasions where it may be appropriate for a medical practitioner to grant both an emergency detention certificate and an incapacity certificate under section 47 of the 2000 Act: for example, where a patient has acute schizophrenia but also has insulin dependent diabetes. For an illustration of this point, see the flowchart at the end of this chapter.

chapter seven

What form of medical examination should the medical practitioner carry out before granting an emergency detention certificate?

30 A medical examination is required for the purpose of deciding whether or not to grant an emergency detention certificate. Best practice would be for such an examination to include:

- a direct, face-to-face, personal examination of the patient;
- a mental state examination;
- an assessment of the patient's decision-making ability and of whether the patient will agree to treatment on a voluntary basis;
- a basic assessment of the patient's physical state in order to help decide whether the patient should be sent to a psychiatric hospital receiving service or to a medical hospital receiving service;
- a basic assessment of the potential risk to the patient and/or others; and
- consideration of as much available and relevant information on the patient's medical and social circumstances as is possible under the circumstances of an emergency, including, where available and practicable, what is contained in past records, case notes as well as the views of carers and any other parties who may be providing care and treatment to the patient.

31 There may be occasions on which it would not be reasonable or practical to carry out such a complete medical examination because the situation presents too great a danger to the practitioner or because the patient will not consent to any form of examination. It would therefore be possible for a patient to be detained after a medical examination carried out by observation only (for example, through a letter box, or a window into a police cell). However, this should only happen where the medical practitioner has first exhausted all other appropriate means of communication with the patient.

32 There may also be occasions on which the medical practitioner may need to consider whether a warrant under section 35 of the Act is required. Such a warrant can be sought by a mental health officer where, for example, a medical practitioner wishes to carry out a medical examination of a mentally disordered person who may be subject or exposed to ill-treatment or neglect but where that practitioner is unable to obtain the consent of that person to the medical examination. Any such warrant, issued by a sheriff or a justice of the peace under section 35(4) of the Act, authorises the detention of the mentally disordered

person for a period of 3 hours for the purpose of carrying out a medical examination. It should be noted that such a warrant does not authorise the person's removal from the premises which they are in at the time of the medical examination. A warrant issued under section 35(4) only authorises the person's detention. Where it is thought likely that the mentally disordered person should be removed from those premises to a place of safety, a warrant should be sought under section 293 of the Act. *For further information on the various warrants available under the Act, see Chapter 15 of Volume 1 of the Code of Practice.*

When must the medical practitioner involve an MHO?

33 Section 36(3)(d) of the Act makes clear that the medical practitioner must consult and seek the consent of an MHO to the granting of the certificate. However, the Act also recognises that there may be occasions where the urgency of the situation is so great that it would not be practicable for such consultation to take place. On such occasions it is permissible for the practitioner to grant the emergency detention certificate without the consent of an MHO.

34 Where the medical practitioner has been able to consult an MHO, it is imperative that the two parties engage in as much joint assessment and consultation as possible with respect to the patient before the certificate is granted. The MHO may be able to provide valuable information regarding, for example, any available alternatives to formal detention; the patient's personal and social circumstances which may have contributed to or caused the current crisis; and the views of the patient's family or carers; etc.

35 A medical practitioner should always make all reasonable efforts to contact an MHO before a certificate is granted. It should be noted that where a certificate is granted without MHO consent, the practitioner must inform hospital managers (who must then inform the Commission and notify the relevant local authority) of the reasons why it was impracticable to consult and seek the consent of an MHO.

36 It would be expected that a medical practitioner would not 'shop around' for an MHO who will consent to the granting of the emergency detention certificate where one MHO has already refused consent. However, to account for a highly exceptional circumstance in which a medical

practitioner wishes to seek a second MHO opinion, it is important that the procedures for and the circumstances in which such a second opinion may be sought are set out in agreed protocols between the local authority and the relevant health partners. In any case where a second MHO assessment is sought, the second MHO should always be informed that another MHO has already refused consent to the granting of the certificate and of the reasons for this refusal.

37 Only where it is impracticable for the medical practitioner to consult an MHO or obtain his/her consent may a medical practitioner grant an emergency detention certificate without any MHO involvement. Such exceptional circumstances could include situations in which:

- there is immediate, serious or life-threatening danger to the patient and/or others around the patient (for example, if the patient is actively threatening violence to others or self-harm);
- no MHO can be contacted; or
- the patient is likely to abscond or has absconded immediately after the medical examination has taken place.

38 Once an emergency detention certificate has been granted, the role of the MHO does not end. The practitioner and all those involved with the patient's care should ensure that the MHO can play as large a role as possible in the entire process. This will ensure that the patient's rights are given the maximum degree of protection possible throughout the detention period and not merely before the certificate is granted. *(Further information on the MHO's role after the certificate has been granted can be found later in this Chapter.)*

What should the MHO take into account when deciding whether or not to consent to the granting of the certificate? What is the role of the MHO if he/she refuses consent?

39 Before the MHO can come to a conclusion on whether or not to consent to the granting of the detention criteria, he/she will need, wherever practicable, to try to elicit the views of the patient with respect to the proposed detention and to any alternative courses of action. The MHO will then need to elicit relevant information about the patient's personal and social circumstances from other mental health professionals who have knowledge of the patient. This could involve a discussion with the medical practitioner about his/her views on why emergency detention is

appropriate; what he/she has observed; why he/she feels that the person's health, safety or welfare or the safety of others is at significant risk as a result of the mental disorder; and why any delay in having recourse to a short-term detention certificate would be undesirable. It will also be important to seek information on such issues from other sources where they are available and where this proves to be practicable. These other sources could include the patient's named person, where the patient already has one, or carers/relatives. Any advance statement, where one exists, should also be considered. All such information will be of relevance not only to the MHO in his/her decision about granting consent but also to the practitioner who is considering whether or not to grant the certificate.

40 Once the MHO is in possession of as much of the above information as is possible and practicable in the circumstances, and once he/she is satisfied that the relevant criteria are met, he/she will need to assess any possible alternatives to the proposed period of formal detention in hospital. He/she should therefore make sure that as many forms of informal and less restrictive treatment as practicable have been explored before consenting to the last resort of compulsory detention.

41 An important consideration for the MHO in deciding whether or not to consent to the granting of the certificate is the likely impact on the person and their carers/family of the emergency detention *not* taking place. The MHO will therefore need to give serious consideration to whether the patient's family/carers, etc are willing and able to continue to care for and support the patient in an appropriate manner, if they have already been involved in doing so, and, if not, whether alternative forms of community-based care and support are appropriate and available.

42 It would be expected that, where practicable, if the patient has been in receipt of mental health services prior to the certificate being granted, members of the multi-disciplinary team providing those services would be consulted. These parties may be able to provide knowledge of the possible and viable alternatives to compulsory powers. They may also need to be involved in planning the patient's care and treatment if the detention certificate is ultimately granted.

chapter seven

43 The MHO should only consent to the detention over the telephone in exceptional circumstances: that is, only where the MHO already has a close knowledge of the patient and the patient's recent case history; or where the MHO has already seen the patient within a short time previous to the medical practitioner's call. (The definition of this time period will necessarily depend on the MHO's judgement within the circumstances of an individual case, but in any case it is unlikely to be more than 48 to 72 hours.)

44 Where the MHO has only been able to give consent over the telephone or has not been able to respond to the medical practitioner's request promptly, he/she should attempt to see the patient as soon as is practicably possible after the certificate has been granted, or arrange for another MHO to do so.

45 In all cases where an MHO has been involved with an emergency detention, best practice would dictate that the MHO should send as soon as practicable a short follow-up report of their involvement and assessment to the patient's RMO and the practitioner who granted the certificate. Such a report will be particularly important in any case where an MHO has withheld consent to the granting of the emergency detention certificate but the certificate was granted all the same. This report could include reference to the actions which the MHO took to ensure, for example, that:

- a discussion took place between the MHO and the practitioner as to the reasons why consent was withheld and why the alternative which the MHO proposed was considered preferable;
- there was a written record of the decision which could be given to the patient's GP, RMO and the Commission;
- there was a viable and safe alternative to detention;
- the practical arrangements to support such an alternative were in place;
- where relevant, others involved with the patient's care and treatment were aware of the alternative and agree their role in any arrangements supporting it; and
- a contingency plan was in place should alternative arrangements break down.

What role is played by the patient's nearest relative or named person before the certificate is granted?

46 The nearest relative plays no formal role in consenting to detention. It is vital to note, however, that a key principle of the Act involves having regard to the views of the patient's carers and their named person as well as any welfare guardian or attorney appointed under the 2000 Act with respect to functions being discharged under the Act. The views of such parties should always therefore be sought, wherever practicable, when a practitioner is discharging a function under this Act.

47 If the patient is entering the mental health service system for the first time when being made subject to a period of emergency detention, it is unlikely that he/she will have already nominated a named person. In such cases, the patient's named person will most likely be their primary carer. However, those medical practitioners, MHOs, and nursing staff subsequently involved with the patient's care and treatment should provide advice to the patient on the role of the named person; on whom he/she might want to have as a named person; and on how to go about nominating a named person.

When and how should the emergency detention certificate be completed?

48 Section 36(12) of the Act provides that the practitioner who grants the detention certificate must have personally examined the patient on the day on which the certificate is granted where the medical examination was completed by 8pm. If the medical examination was completed after 8pm, then the certificate must be granted within 4 hours. It should also be noted that the initial examination of the patient may not be carried out by one practitioner, and then the certificate granted by another.

chapter seven

Processes following the granting of the emergency detention certificate

Transferring the patient to hospital

49 It would be expected that responsibility for organising the patient's transfer to hospital would be assumed by the medical practitioner who granted the emergency detention certificate. Where the medical practitioner is unable to organise the patient's transfer him/herself, he/she should take all reasonable steps to ensure that the transfer and admission to hospital is taken care of by another person/party. This is likely to be the Ambulance Service, a psychiatric nurse or other mental health professional.

50 Where the medical practitioner assumes overall responsibility for the organisation of the transfer, it should be remembered by the other parties involved in the patient's transfer that the practitioner will likely have no control over the means of transferring the patient. The other parties involved in the transfer, particularly those who do control the means by which the patient is transferred, should therefore co-operate as fully as possible with the medical practitioner to ensure that the transfer takes place as swiftly and as smoothly as possible.

51 A hospital or other service should never demand that a medical practitioner grant an emergency detention certificate as a prerequisite to obtaining transport to hospital and/or an escort. Receiving hospitals or other services should assess requests for admission, transport and escort on the basis of need alone and separately from any considerations of whether or not compulsory powers have been granted or are likely to be granted.

52 Although the Act provides for a 72 hour period during which the patient may be transferred to hospital, it would be extremely rare for the full 72 hour period to be required except in the most exceptional circumstances. Such circumstances would be most likely to arise in rural or remote environments. In all cases, however, the patient should be transferred to hospital as quickly as practicable and should be cared for within the least restrictive, safest and most therapeutic environment possible. If the transfer is unduly delayed, the assessment of the patient's mental health and the provision of beneficial care and treatment will also be unduly delayed.

53 If it is predicted that there will be a considerable delay before the transfer to hospital can proceed (for example, because the patient must be conveyed from an island setting to a distant psychiatric facility), consideration should be given to the use of other facilities such as community hospitals or treatment centres, particularly where the delay is likely to extend overnight. It should be noted, however, that where a patient is admitted to hospital (whether it be a community hospital or psychiatric hospital), the 72 hour period during which the patient may be removed to hospital ends, and the 72 hour period of emergency detention begins.

54 Holding a patient in a police car, police van or another location such as a police cell for lengthy periods should be avoided other than in the most exceptional circumstances of physical risk.

55 Wherever possible, a patient should always be accompanied by and/or supervised by at least one suitably trained health care professional. Every effort should be made to comfort and reassure the patient during the transfer process.

56 Because of the nature of the situation, emergency detentions can easily become public events. It would therefore be good practice to take all reasonable steps to ensure that the transfer and detention proceedings are conducted with as low a profile as is possible under the circumstances so as to preserve the privacy and dignity of the individual involved. For example, marked police vehicles and ambulances can be parked within easy reach of, but not necessarily in immediate proximity to the emergency scene, ready to respond quickly if and when they are required. In all cases, regard should be had to the principle of least restrictive alternative.

57 All the parties involved with the transfer procedure should also be particularly sensitive towards the needs of carers and other family members in such situations. Local authorities and, consequently, MHOs will also need to be conscious of their responsibilities under the National Assistance Act 1948 with respect to the preservation of the patient's property and should also consider the needs of any dependants and pets. The possible existence of an advance statement made by the patient should be considered, as far as is possible under the circumstances, as there may be particular treatment issues that the patient would want practitioners to have regard to.

chapter seven

Development of Psychiatric Emergency Plans

58 As a means of addressing all these issues comprehensively and in a manner which best reflects local circumstances, it would be best practice for the relevant local agencies and service providers who might potentially be involved in psychiatric emergencies to work together to develop and agree on a "Psychiatric Emergency Plan" (PEP). This would allow potential local difficulties to be addressed and contingency procedures put in place before they arise for real. The aim of a PEP would be to agree on procedures which would manage the transfer and detention process in a manner which minimises distress, disturbance and risk for the patient and others and which ensures as smooth and safe a transition as possible from the site of the emergency to the appropriate treatment setting. The professionals involved in the drawing up of a PEP could include, but should not necessarily be limited to, general practitioners, approved medical practitioners, MHOs, other social workers, social care workers, CPNs, ward nursing staff, independent service providers, police officers, and ambulance personnel. It will also be important to seek input into the preparation of a PEP from mental health service users and carers.

59 It would be best practice to use a PEP as a basis for joint training of all those professionals named in the plan as having specific responsibilities in the transfer and detention process. Similarly, it would be best practice to ensure that the PEP is updated regularly to ensure its relevance and robustness, particularly in light of any significant incident.

Admitting the patient to hospital

60 A patient's initial experience of hospital and of detention can be influenced considerably by the procedures involved with admission to hospital. This is particularly the case where the patient is being admitted in an emergency. An emergency admission can be a highly distressing and traumatic procedure for the patient, sometimes as traumatic as the patient's condition itself. All those involved with the patient's care and treatment will need to keep in mind the possibility that the patient may well retain significant insight into the condition and its implications and/or into other important aspects of their lives. Hospital staff should also bear in mind that patients will often have considerable anxieties about the practical considerations which they have left behind at home, such as dependants, pets etc. Although hospital staff are not directly concerned

with such issues, they should nonetheless take the patient's concerns seriously, be willing to discuss them and provide relevant assistance via the relevant bodies or organisations, wherever practicable.

61 Patients should be treated with as much sensitivity as possible and afforded the greatest degree of privacy achievable under the circumstances of an emergency. Wherever possible, a member of the ward staff should be available to explain all relevant procedures to the patient. In this connection, it would always be good practice for a patient to be allocated a named nurse on admission. It would also be good practice for a hospital to provide each patient with an information pack on admission to hospital. This would be written in plain English (as well as being made available in other languages) and could cover, for example, details of any restrictions the patient will face in hospital; possible side effects of medications; where to find public telephones in the hospital, etc.

62 In this connection, practitioners are reminded of the duties placed on hospital managers by section 260 of the Act to provide the patient with information on a range of issues such as, for example, the power of the RMO with respect to revoking the detention certificate and the consequences of the operation of the provision under which the patient is detained. Similarly, section 261 places duties on the hospital managers to take all reasonable steps to secure for the patient assistance in overcoming communication difficulties.

Duties of the medical practitioner who granted the emergency detention certificate

63 The medical practitioner who granted the emergency detention certificate must ensure that the certificate is passed to the managers of the hospital in which the patient is to be detained. Section 36(7) of the Act makes clear that the patient's detention in hospital is only authorised if the certificate has been given to the hospital managers before the patient is admitted. The actual person(s) in an individual hospital who may perform the function of receiving the certificate on behalf of the hospital managers should be clearly designated and identified by those managers.

chapter seven

64 Section 37 of the Act makes clear that the practitioner who granted the emergency detention certificate must give notice to the managers of the hospital in which the patient is detained of a range of matters. Those matters are:

- the reason for granting the certificate;
- whether the consent of an MHO was obtained to the granting of the certificate;
- if the certificate was granted without consent to its granting having been obtained from an MHO, the reason why it was impracticable to consult an MHO; and
- the alternatives to granting the certificate which were considered by the medical practitioner and the reason(s) why the medical practitioner determined that these alternatives were inappropriate.

65 The practitioner must provide this notification to the hospital managers when they receive the emergency detention certificate. If s/he cannot provide this notification at that point, he/she must do so as soon as is reasonably practicable after that point. Although the Act states that the certifying practitioner must give this information to the hospital managers, it would still be acceptable for the practitioner to entrust the detention certificate to the person in charge of the patient's escort to hospital and for them to deliver it to the hospital managers.

66 The medical practitioner should also be fully involved with the processes allied to transferring the patient to hospital, where relevant, as described in paragraphs 49 and 57 above.

What is the role of the MHO after the certificate has been granted?

67 It would be best practice for the MHO to send to the practitioner who granted the certificate and to the approved medical practitioner appointed as the patient's RMO, a written record of his/her involvement with the detention process. This record would be particularly important in cases where the MHO did not have the opportunity to interview the patient prior to it being granted.

68 Where the MHO has given his/her consent to the detention, he/she will want to ensure that a range of actions take place. These actions are in addition to and complementary to any which ward staff may carry out but will necessarily vary according to the circumstances of the individual patient. The MHO will wish to take all reasonable steps to ensure:

- that the patient is aware of his/her status and rights;
- that the patient has access to information on representation and advocacy and where necessary, provide assistance in making contact with these services;
- that the patient has access to interpretation and translation services, or services that address other communication needs;
- the safety of any children or other dependants or those in the patient's care;
- the safety of any pets;
- the security of the patient's premises and belongings if the patient has been detained at home and force was required to enter the premises;
- that the patient's named person and/or nearest relative has been informed and has the MHO's contact details;
- that the ward medical staff are aware of the patient's views on consent to treatment, including the existence and content of any advance statement made by the patient;
- that the ward medical staff have contact details of the MHO and of the patient's named person/carers, etc;
- that a written record of the MHO's decision to give consent is included in the patient's records, wherever practicable; and
- that the patient and his/her carers and dependants have the MHO's contact details.

69 The MHO should also be fully involved with the processes allied to transferring the patient to hospital, where relevant, as described in paragraphs 49 to 57 above.

Duties of hospital managers

70 The Act imposes a range of duties on the relevant hospital managers where a patient becomes subject to an emergency detention certificate.

71 Section 38 also places a duty on hospital managers to ensure that the patient is examined by an approved medical practitioner as soon as is practicable and appropriate after the patient's admission to hospital. (It

may, of course, be additionally necessary for the patient to be examined by a specialist in physical disorders.) The purpose of such an examination is to ensure that the patient is examined by a specialist in psychiatry as soon as possible after admission in order to review the ongoing need for detention.

72 If, as a result of this review, the AMP is not satisfied that the relevant detention criteria continue to be met, he/she must revoke the certificate and follow the procedures set out in sections 39 and 40 of the Act. If the AMP is satisfied that the relevant detention criteria continue to be met, he/she should give consideration to revoking the emergency detention certificate as soon as practicable and to granting a short-term detention certificate where the practitioner believes it would be appropriate to do so and where the relevant criteria are met.

73 Where the emergency detention certificate was granted without an MHO having been consulted, it would be best practice for the approved medical practitioner carrying out the initial examination of the patient to contact and consult an MHO with respect to the detention certificate as soon as is practicable.

74 Even before this examination by an approved medical practitioner, however, it would be expected that the medical practitioner admitting the patient to hospital would assess whether the patient's mental state is such as to justify the continued operation of the emergency detention certificate. Where he/she believes that the detention criteria are no longer met, he/she should bring these views to the attention of an approved medical practitioner as quickly as is possible so that the approved medical practitioner can consider whether the emergency detention certificate needs to be revoked.

75 There may be occasions where an approved medical practitioner has some concerns about the reasons why the emergency detention certificate was initially granted. It would be best practice for the approved medical practitioner to bring any such concerns to the attention of the Mental Welfare Commission to allow them to contact the certifying practitioner for a fuller discussion of the circumstances surrounding the detention.

76 Section 260 of the Act places a duty on the managers of the hospital to which the patient is admitted to provide the patient with a range of information which principally relates to the patient's rights. Section 261 similarly places duties on those hospital managers to provide the patient with assistance in overcoming communications problems.

77 Section 230 obliges hospital managers to appoint an approved medical practitioner to act as the patient's RMO as soon as is practicable after the granting of the emergency detention certificate. Acute medical and surgical hospital management services will need to enter into local arrangements with psychiatric providers to ensure the availability of approved medical practitioners to act as the RMO for such a patient. *(For further information on this, see Chapter 11 of this Volume of the Code of Practice.)* Where it is practicable, it would be best practice for the approved medical practitioner appointed as the patient's RMO to be the same practitioner who examined the patient as soon as practicable after admission to hospital.

Who must the hospital managers notify that the detention has taken place?

78 In terms of section 38(3)(a) of the Act, the managers of the hospital in which the patient is detained must inform a range of parties that the emergency detention certificate has been granted within 12 hours of their receiving the certificate. Such informing will most likely be carried by telephone. The parties are:

- the patient's nearest relative;
- any person who lives with the patient, if the patient's nearest relative does not live with the patient;
- the patient's named person, if the hospital managers know who the named person is; and
- the Commission.

79 Hospital managers must also give notice to the parties listed in the preceding paragraph of the information set out at section 38(3)(b)(i) within 7 days of their receiving it from the practitioner who granted the certificate. The information in section 38(3)(b)(i) is that which is described in paragraph 64 above. Additionally, in a situation where the certificate was granted without the consent of an MHO, hospital managers must give this notice to the local authority for the area in which the patient lives or to the local authority for the area where the hospital is situated if the managers do not know where the patient lives.

chapter seven

Which forms of treatment may be administered during a period of emergency detention?

80 The granting of an emergency detention certificate does not give general authority to provide compulsory medical treatment for mental disorder under Part 16 of the Act. Medical treatment for a mental disorder during a period of emergency detention will normally require either the consent of the patient; authority under the Adults with Incapacity (Scotland) Act 2000; or, in the case of a child, the consent of the child in terms of the Age of Legal Capacity (Scotland) Act 1991 and the Children (Scotland) Act 1995.

81 Urgent medical treatment for a mental disorder may, however, be administered under the terms of section 243 of the Act to any patient whose detention in hospital is authorised by an emergency detention certificate. Such treatment can be administered to the patient even where the patient does not consent to the treatment or is incapable of consenting to the treatment.

82 *For further information on urgent medical treatment and section 243 of the Act, see Chapter 10 of Volume 1 of the Code of Practice.*

Revoking an emergency detention certificate (sections 39 and 40)

83 Sections 39 and 40 of the Act set out the procedures to be followed where an approved medical practitioner revokes an emergency detention certificate. A certificate must be revoked under two sets of circumstances. These circumstances are:

- where the practitioner is not satisfied that it continues to be necessary for the patient's detention in hospital to be authorised by the emergency detention certificate (in other words, the practitioner is not satisfied that the patient needs to be treated on a compulsory basis); or
- where the practitioner is not satisfied that the conditions at section 36(4)(a) and (b) and (5)(b) continue to be met in respect of the patient. (These conditions are firstly, that the patient has a mental disorder; secondly, that the patient's decision-making ability with respect to medical treatment for mental disorder is significantly impaired by that mental disorder; and thirdly, that there would be a significant risk to the health, safety or welfare of the patient or to the safety of any other person if the patient were not detained in hospital.)

84 Where either of these two sets of circumstances apply, the practitioner must revoke the certificate.

chapter seven

85 Where a practitioner revokes an emergency detention certificate, a range of notification procedures must be complied with. These are set out in section 40 of the Act. The practitioner must inform the patient and the managers of the hospital in which the patient is detained as soon as practicable after revoking the certificate. Those hospital managers must then inform the following parties of the revocation as soon as practicable after being informed by the approved medical practitioner. These parties are:

- the patient's nearest relative;
- any person who resides with the patient if the patient's nearest relative does not reside with the patient;
- the patient's named person if the hospital managers know who the named person is and if the named person is not covered by the two preceding categories;
- the Commission;
- if the managers know where the patient resides, the local authority for the area in which the patient resides; and
- if the managers do not know where the patient resides, the local authority for the area in which the hospital is situated.

Suspending an emergency detention certificate (sections 41 and 42)

86 Where a patient is subject to an emergency detention certificate and is detained in hospital on the authority of that certificate, it is possible to suspend that authorisation of the patient's detention in hospital for a limited period of time without revoking the emergency detention certificate itself. Under such circumstances, section 41 of the Act allows for a "suspension certificate" to be granted. Such a certificate can only be granted by the patient's RMO.

How long can a suspension certificate last?

87 A suspension certificate can last for any period of time which the patient's RMO stipulates. In terms of section 41(2), this period may be the duration of an event or series of events with or without any associated travel. By implication, the time and date on which this suspension certificate is due to expire may not go beyond the time and date on which the emergency detention certificate is due to expire.

Can conditions be attached to a suspension certificate?

88 Yes. The patient's RMO may attach conditions to the suspension certificate by virtue of section 41(3) and (4) of the Act. Such conditions may be:

- that the patient be kept in the charge of a person authorised in writing for that purpose by the patient's RMO; or
- any other conditions which the patient's RMO wishes to specify.

89 The patient's RMO can only grant any such conditions where, in terms of section 41(3) of the Act, he/she considers them to be in the interests of the patient or necessary for the protection of any other person. It should be noted that the RMO's giving of authority to another person to keep a patient in his/her charge can only be done in writing.

90 Examples of conditions which could be attached to a suspension certificate include that the patient live in a specified place under the care of a specified person; be kept in the charge of an escorting nurse; or that the patient accept visits from a medical practitioner or an MHO. It would be expected that the RMO informs the patient's MHO and other members of the multi-disciplinary team of any conditions attached to the suspension certificate, and that he/she ensures that procedures and contingency plans are put in place for any occasion where the conditions are not complied with.

When would it be appropriate to grant a suspension certificate?

91 Given the brevity of a period of emergency detention, there are unlikely to be many occasions or events which would require a patient's attendance in person outwith the hospital in which they have been detained but which would not require the emergency detention certificate itself to be revoked. It would be expected, however, that before a suspension certificate is granted under section 41 the RMO would carry out as full an assessment as possible of the potential risk to the health and welfare of the patient and/or others (for example, carers, family members or accompanying staff) of granting the suspension certificate. Such an assessment should only be carried out after as full a consultation as possible has taken place with the other members of the multi-disciplinary team providing care and treatment to the patient.

92 Practitioners are also reminded that they should have regard to the principles of the Act and other matters laid out in sections 1 to 3, when deciding whether or not to grant a suspension certificate. Particularly important in this connection will be the principle stated at section 1(4) of the Act which provides that any person discharging a function under the Act must discharge that function in the manner which "involves the minimum restriction on the freedom of the patient that is necessary in the circumstances".

93 Before granting a suspension certificate (for example, for the purpose of allowing the patient to attend a funeral of a close relative), the RMO and the multi-disciplinary team will need to balance an acknowledgement of the social and emotional importance of attending such an event against the likely impact of attendance on the symptoms and behaviours related to the patient's mental disorder. This is particularly important given that these symptoms and behaviours had after all dictated that it was

"necessary as a matter of urgency to detain the patient in hospital" when the emergency detention certificate was first granted. Similarly, cognisance will have to be taken of the views of others (family, carers, friends, etc), who may also be involved in the event, on the patient's proposed attendance.

94 A suspension certificate should only be granted in relation to the assessed needs of the patient and not as a method of managing beds in wards which are running at or above capacity. A decision to suspend the power to detain the patient in hospital should only ever be taken where it is in the best interests of the patient.

Who is responsible for the patient's care and treatment while subject to a suspension certificate?

95 The patient's RMO remains responsible for the patient's care and treatment while the patient is subject to a suspension certificate. He/she must therefore ensure that appropriate arrangements are made or have been made for the patient's care and treatment while not in hospital. It should also be remembered that the duty under section 1(6) of the Act to provide "appropriate services" to the patient applies to any time where the patient is subject to a suspension certificate.

96 It will always be important to ensure that clear and effective communication channels exist between the patient, relatives and/or carers (especially where the patient is residing with them for the duration of the suspension certificate), members of the patient's multi-disciplinary team and the RMO so that the patient's progress towards recovery can be effectively monitored and acted upon, where appropriate.

What should happen where a patient requires medical treatment in another hospital?

97 There may be occasions where a patient detained in hospital on the authority of an emergency detention certificate requires to be transferred urgently to another hospital, for example, to receive treatment for a physical disorder. (Note that only urgent treatment for mental disorder can be administered to a patient subject to an emergency detention certificate under section 243 of the Act: an emergency detention certificate does not give practitioners a general authority to treat under Part 16 of the Act.) A suspension certificate would not have to be granted in such

circumstances as no hospital is specified in an emergency detention certificate. Best practice would suggest, however, that the RMO take steps to ensure that the patient's named person, primary carer, MHO and other relevant members of the multi-disciplinary team are informed of any such emergency transfer as soon as possible after it becomes apparent that the transfer may be necessary.

Can a suspension certificate be revoked?

98 It may be necessary for the patient's RMO to revoke a suspension certificate granted under section 41 of the Act. He/she may revoke the certificate where he/she is satisfied that it is necessary in the interests of the patient to do so or that it is necessary for the protection of any other person to do so. Where an RMO revokes a suspension certificate, he/she must in terms of section 42(3) of the Act inform a range of parties of the revocation as soon as practicable after it has taken place. These parties are:

- the patient;
- any person who had been authorised by the RMO to keep the patient in his/her charge for the duration of the suspension certificate; and
- the managers of the hospital in which the patient is detained.

99 It would also be best practice for the RMO to inform the patient's MHO and the other members of the patient's multi-disciplinary team of the revocation of the suspension certificate.

100 Those hospital managers must then in terms of section 42(4) of the Act inform a further group of parties of the revocation. These parties are:

- the patient's nearest relative;
- any person who resides with the patient assuming that the nearest relative does not live with the patient;
- the patient's named person assuming that the managers know who the named person is and that the named person is not the patient's nearest relative or a person who resides with the patient;
- the Commission;
- if the managers know where the patient resides, the local authority for the area in which the patient resides; and
- if the managers do not know where the patient resides, the local authority for the area in which the hospital is situated.

chapter seven

Guide for medical practitioners on the granting of an emergency detention certificate under section 36 of the Mental Health (Care and Treatment) (Scotland) Act 2003

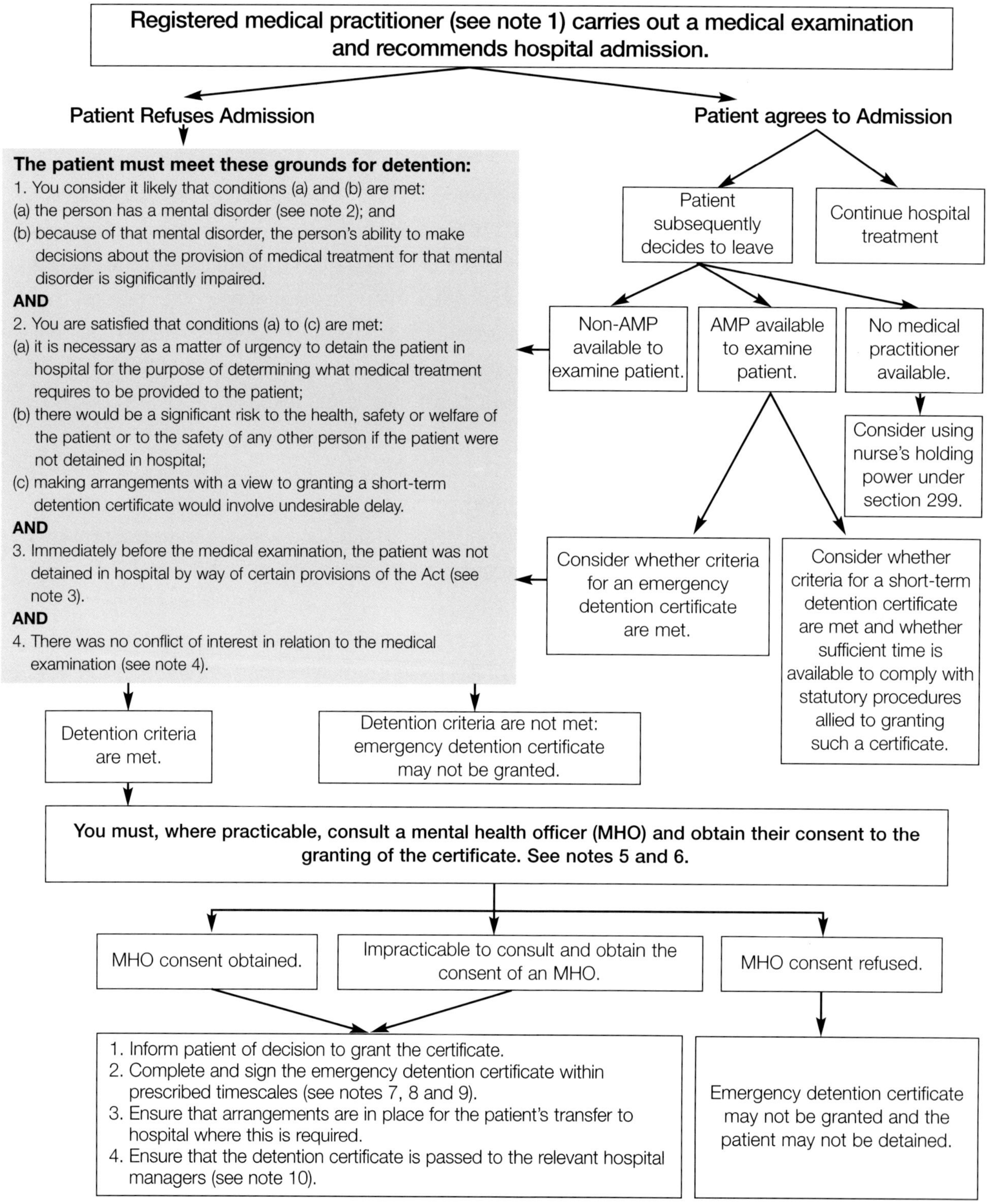

Throughout the process of granting an emergency detention certificate, you are bound to have regard to the principles of the legislation as laid out in sections 1 to 3 of the Act.

chapter seven

Notes on the procedures to be followed by medical practitioners when granting an emergency detention certificate.

Note 1: Any registered medical practitioner may grant an emergency detention certificate. You do not have to be an "approved medical practitioner" ("AMP"). (An AMP is a term particular to the Act. It is a medical practitioner who has been approved by a Health Board under section 22 of this Act and who has "special experience in the diagnosis and treatment of mental disorder". An AMP will therefore normally be a psychiatrist).

Note 2: Section 328(1) of the Act defines "mental disorder" as "mental illness, personality disorder or learning disability, however caused or manifested". Section 328(2) further states that a person is not mentally disordered by reason only of sexual orientation; sexual deviancy; trans-sexualism; transvestism; dependence on, or use of alcohol or drugs; behaviour that causes, or is likely to cause, harassment, alarm or distress to an other person; or acting as no prudent person would act.

Note 3: The relevant provisions are set out at section 36(2) of the Act and they are:

- an emergency detention certificate;
- a short-term detention certificate;
- an extension certificate issued under section 47 of the Act pending an application for a CTO;
- section 68 of the Act (i.e. the extension to the detention period authorised once a CTO application has been submitted to the Tribunal);
- a certificate granted under sections 114(2) or 115(2) of the Act (i.e. a certificate issued subsequent to a patient's non-compliance with the terms of a community-based interim CTO or a CTO).

Note 4: Regulations have not been made for conflict of interest in connection with the emergency detention certificate.

Note 5: The medical practitioner must consult and seek the consent of an MHO to the granting of the certificate. All reasonable efforts should be made to contact an MHO. However, where the urgency of the situation is so great that it would not be practicable for this consultation to take place then it is permissible for the practitioner to grant the EDC without consent. Best practice would suggest that the most suitable medical practitioner to grant the emergency detention certificate is the medical practitioner within the multi-disciplinary team responsible for the patient's care.

Note 6: Best practice would be that if one MHO refuses to grant consent, then the medical practitioner should take account of the exceptional circumstances in which a second opinion is required. It is important that the procedures are agreed between the local authority and relevant health partners.

Note 7: A valid emergency detention certificate can be issued on any document if form DET 1 is not available. However it is strongly recommended that the form be used in all circumstances. If form DET 1 is not used, the emergency detention certificate must state the practitioner's reasons for believing the conditions mentioned at points 1 and 2 be met and must be signed by the medical practitioner.

All non-statutory forms may be found on the Scottish Executive's website www.scotland.gov.uk/health/mentalhealthlaw

Note 8: The emergency detention certificate must be completed either by the end of the day on which the medical examination takes place (if the examination takes place before 8pm) or within 4 hours of the medical examination being completed (if it takes place after 8pm).

Note 9: The emergency detention certificate authorises, firstly, the patient's transfer to hospital within 72 hours of the certificate being granted; and, secondly, the patient's detention in hospital for 72 hours.

Note 10: Section 36(7) of the Act states that the patient's detention in hospital is only authorised if the emergency detention certificate is given to the managers of the hospital before the patient is admitted to hospital under the authority of the certificate. If the patient is already in hospital when the certificate is granted, then the certificate must be given to the hospital managers as soon as practicable after it was granted.

chapter seven

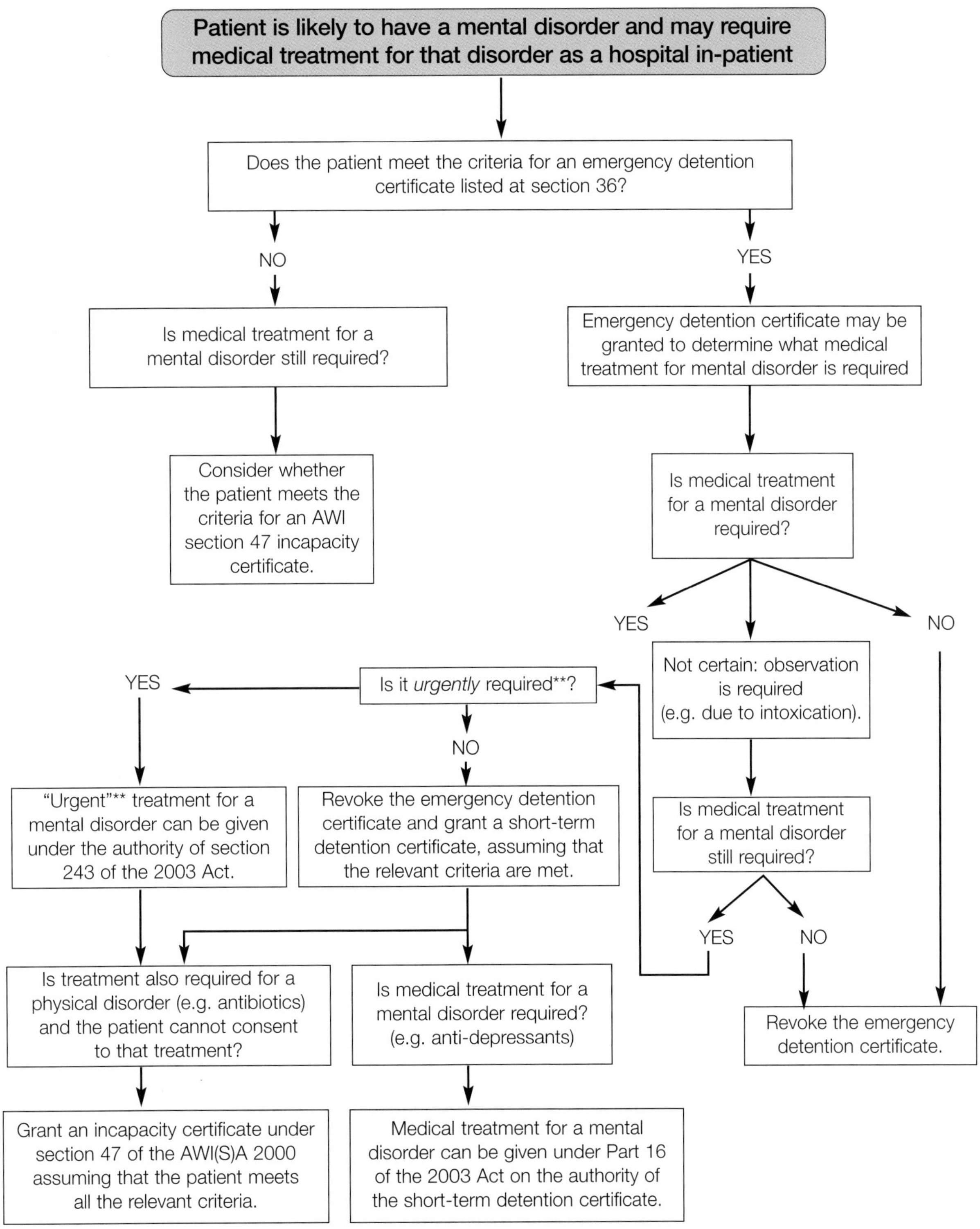

** "Urgent" means in this context: in order to save the patient's life; to prevent serious deterioration in the patient's condition; to alleviate serious suffering on the part of the patient; or to prevent the patient from behaving violently or being a danger to him/herself or others.

chapter 8
absconding (part 20)

chapter eight

Introduction

This chapter deals with the provisions laid out in Part 20 of the Act which relate to patients who abscond while subject to certain compulsory powers under the Act. (Under the Mental Health (Scotland) Act 1984, absconding was often referred to as "absence without leave". Under the Act, absconding is also sometimes referred to as "a period of unauthorised absence".) The specific compulsory powers referred to in this chapter are set out in the table after paragraph 2. Broadly speaking, however, these powers are emergency and short-term detention certificates and compulsory treatment orders. For information on the provisions of the Act which relate to absconding mentally disordered offenders, please see Chapter 6 part 1 of Volume 3, of the Code of Practice.

This chapter describes, firstly, which patients can be made subject to the Act's absconding provisions before describing, and secondly, the procedures to be followed once a patient has absconded. The chapter then moves on to a discussion of the effect of a period of unauthorised absence on the expiry date of certain detention certificates and orders. Finally, the issue of patients who abscond from other jurisdictions is considered.

Overview of absconding provisions

01 The provisions of section 303 of the Act or paragraphs 10 to 14 of this chapter set out the procedures to be followed when certain patients abscond. The categories of patients who may be made subject to these provisions are set out in sections 301 and 302 of the Act and in the table after paragraph 2 of this chapter. The remainder of the chapter focuses on the statutory procedures which must be followed under the Act subsequent to a patient absconding.

chapter eight

Which categories of patients can be said to have absconded

02 These categories are set out in sections 301 and 302 of the Act. Section 301 sets out the various categories of patients who are subject to a CTO while section 302 describes the other categories of patients. The table overleaf describes the circumstances in which a patient can be said to have absconded when subject to certain compulsory powers. In any case where the patient has absconded, the patient is liable to be taken into custody and dealt with in accordance with the provisions of section 303.

Compulsory measure to which a patient is subject	When can a patient be said to have absconded while subject to that compulsory measure and when can the provisions of section 303 be invoked?
Emergency detention certificate	If the patient absconds from any place where he/she is being kept pending removal to hospital under the certificate. If the patient absconds from the hospital in which he/she is detained under that certificate.
Emergency detention certificate in respect of which a suspension certificate has been granted under section 41(1)	If a condition has been added to that suspension certificate that the patient be kept in the charge of an authorised person or that the patient reside at a specified place either continuously, for or at specified times.If the patient absconds from the charge of that authorised person or fails to comply with that residence condition, then he/she has absconded; or If a condition has been added to the suspension certificate requiring the patient on being recalled or on the expiry of the period specified in the certificate to return to the hospital in which the patient was detained or to go to another place and the patient fails to comply with that condition then he/she has absconded.
Short-term detention certificate	If the patient absconds from any place where he/she is being kept pending removal to hospital under the certificate. If the patient absconds from the hospital in which he/she is detained under that certificate.
Short-term detention certificate in respect of which a suspension certificate has been granted under section 53(1)	If a condition has been added to that suspension certificate that the patient be kept in the charge of an authorised person or that the patient reside at a specified place either continuously, for or at specified times.If the patient absconds from the charge of that authorised person or fails to comply with that condition, they wil bc considered to have absconded. If a condition has been added to the suspension certificate requiring the patient on being recalled or on the expiry of the period specified in the certificate to return to the hospital in which the patient was detained or to go to another place and the patient fails to comply with that condition then he/she has absconded.

chapter eight

Compulsory measure to which a patient is subject	When can a patient be said to have absconded while subject to that compulsory measure and when can the provisions of section 303 be invoked?
Extension certificate	If the patient absconds from any place where he/she is being kept pending removal to hospital under the certificate. If the patient absconds from the hospital in which he/she is detained under that certificate.
Section 68 (i.e. the 5 working days' period of detention subsequent to a CTO application being made)	If the patient absconds from any place where he/she is being kept pending removal to hospital under the provision. If the patient absconds from the hospital in which he/she is detained under that provision.
Compulsory treatment order or interim compulsory treatment order authorising treatment in hospital	If the patient absconds from that hospital. If the patient absconds from any place where he/she is being kept pending removal to hospital.
Compulsory treatment order authorising treatment in hospital	If the patient absconds while being removed to hospital or while being transferred to another hospital in Scotland under section 124 of the Act.
Compulsory treatment order or an interim compulsory treatment order which authorises treatment in hospital but in respect of which a suspension certificate has been granted under section 127(1) or (3)	If a condition has been added to that suspension certificate that the patient be kept in the charge of an authorised person or that he/she resides at a specified place either continuously, for or at specified times.If the patient absconds from the charge of that authorised person or fails to comply with that residence condition, then he/she has absconded. If a condition has been added to this suspension certificate that the patient must return to the hospital specified in the CTO or must go to some other specified place upon being recalled or upon the expiry of a specified period or upon or after the occurrence of a specified event.If that patient fails to comply with such a condition, then the patient has absconded.
Compulsory treatment order or interim compulsory treatment order which specifies a "residence requirement" by way of section 66(1)(e)	If the patient fails to comply with that residence requirement.

Compulsory measure to which a patient is subject	When can a patient be said to have absconded while subject to that compulsory measure and when can the provisions of section 303 be invoked?
Compulsory treatment order which specifies the requirement to obtain the MHO's approval to any proposed change of address by way of section 66(1)(g)	If the patient fails to comply with that requirement.
Detention under section 113(5) of the Act (i.e. the period of 72 hour detention which immediately follows non-compliance with a community-based CTO or interim CTO)	If the patient absconds from any place where he/she is being kept pending removal to hospital under that provision. If the patient absconds from the hospital in which he/she is detained under that provision.
A certificate issued under sections 114(2) or 115(2) of the Act (i.e. a certificate which authorises the patient's detention in hospital if the patient has not complied with certain of the compulsory measures specified in a community-based CTO or community-based interim CTO)	If the patient absconds from any place where he/she is being kept pending removal to hospital under that certificate. If the patient absconds from the hospital in which he/she is detained under that certificate.
Section 299 of the Act (i.e. where a patient is detained in hospital as a result of a nurse's holding power)	If the patient absconds from any place where he/she is being kept pending removal to hospital under this power. If the patient absconds from the hospital in which he/she is detained under this power.

What should happen once a patient has absconded?

03 Where a patient has absconded, sections 301 and 302 of the Act state that the patient is liable to be taken into custody and dealt with in accordance with the provisions of section 303. The provisions of that section are described in paragraphs 10 to 14 below.

04 It would be expected that the decision as to whether the patient is liable to be taken into custody is recorded within the patient's medical notes with respect to issues such as who took the decision; who was consulted before the decision was taken; and on what evidence the decision was taken. Indeed, it would be best practice for the patient's multi-disciplinary team to be the forum in which such a decision would be taken.

chapter eight

05 This transparency around the decision-making process will be particularly important where the patient was subject to community-based measures when he/she was deemed to have been liable to be taken into custody. In such cases, the patient should be afforded as full an opportunity as possible to explain why, in terms of section 301(3) for example, he/she has not complied with the requirement to reside at a specified place before the decision is taken that he/she is liable to be taken into custody. It will also be important in such circumstances to have regard to the principles and other matters set out in sections 1 to 3 of the Act, particularly the principle stated at section 1(4) with respect to discharging functions under the Act in a manner "that involves the minimum restriction on the freedom of the patient that is necessary in the circumstances."

What is the difference between the absconding provisions in Part 20 and the provisions on breaching a community-based CTO in Part 7 Chapter 5?

06 It may appear that there is some overlap between the provisions of the Act which relate to a patient's non-compliance with a community-based CTO or interim CTO (as set out in Part 7 Chapter 5 of the Act or Chapter 6 of this Volume of the Code of Practice) and the provisions of the Act relating to patients who abscond while subject to a community-based CTO or interim CTO. For example, where a patient fails to comply with a "residency requirement" specified in an order (that is, the requirement at section 66(1)(e)), it would be possible to invoke either the provisions of Part 7 Chapter 5 or the absconding provisions of Part 20 with respect to the patient's non-compliance.

07 In deciding which set of provisions is most appropriate to invoke with respect to this non-compliance, it is important to bear in mind the powers which the provisions confer and the range of parties on whom they are conferred. For example, if the provisions of Part 7 Chapter 5 were to be invoked with respect to a patient who does not comply with a residency requirement, the patient's RMO would have the power to take the patient into custody by way of section 113(4) and to detain him/her for up to 72 hours with a view to carrying out a medical examination. It is likely that this power would be exercised where the detention of the patient in hospital on a longer-term basis by way of sections 114(2) or 115(2) was being considered. If, under the same circumstances, the provisions of Part 20 were to be invoked, then a range of parties

(including the patient's MHO, a police constable, and any other person authorised by the RMO) could take the patient into custody and return him/her to the address from which he/she has absconded.

08 Given the differences between the powers conferred by the provisions of Part 7 Chapter 5 and Part 20, the following factors may well need to be taken into account when deciding which set of provisions should be invoked. Firstly, which party is making the decision? This is because only the patient's RMO is empowered to take the patient into custody or to authorise another person to take the patient into custody under the provisions of Part 7 Chapter 5 whereas a wider range of parties are empowered to take the person into custody under Part 20. Secondly, the powers under Part 20 are time-limited in as much as the patient may not be taken into custody if he/she has absconded (i.e. breached the residency requirement in this example) for a period of greater than 3 months. The provisions of Part 7 Chapter 5 are not time-limited. Thirdly, taking a patient into custody under the powers granted by Part 7 Chapter 5 allows the further detention of the patient in hospital for up to 72 hours and is likely to be done with a view to applying additional detention powers under sections 114(2) or 115(2) of the Act and with a view to considering whether the patient's CTO needs to be varied to specify detention in hospital rather than community-based compulsory measures. The purpose of taking a patient into custody under the powers granted by Part 20 is principally to return the patient to the place from which they absconded rather than to pursue further actions. Although much will depend on the individual circumstances of the patient, it may be more appropriate to invoke the powers under Part 20 where the person exercising that power believes that the patient's non-compliance with the residency requirement is only a "temporary blip" and that the measures authorised in the patient's CTO do not need to be varied.

09 In deciding which set of powers to invoke, it is vital that the relevant parties have regard for the principle set out at section 1(4) of the Act: that is, the principle that the patient should be treated in a manner which invokes the minimum restriction on his/her freedom that is necessary in the circumstances. Furthermore, as much consultation as is practicable under the circumstances should take place between the relevant members of the patient's multi-disciplinary team and the patient's carers and/or relevant relatives before any decision is made as to which set of powers to invoke.

chapter eight

Which actions can be taken subsequent to a patient absconding?

10 Section 303 of the Act sets out the procedures to be followed once a patient has absconded. In terms of subsection (1) of that section, the following actions may be taken:

- the absconding patient can be taken into custody;
- the absconding patient can be returned or taken to the hospital in which he/she was detained or was to be detained. If this is not appropriate or practicable, the patient may alternatively be taken to any other place which is considered appropriate by the patient's RMO;
- the absconding patient may be returned to or taken to any other place which he/she absconded from or where he/she failed to reside. If this is not appropriate or practicable, the patient may alternatively be taken to any other place which is considered appropriate by the patient's RMO.

11 The persons who are allowed to carry out the actions described in section 303(1) of the Act or paragraph 10 above are set out in section 303(3). They are:

- a mental health officer;
- a police constable;
- a member of staff of any hospital;
- a member of staff of the establishment where the patient is required to reside as a result of a residence requirement being specified in a CTO; and
- any other person who has been authorised to carry out any of the above actions by the patient's RMO.

12 With respect to the final bullet-point in the previous paragraph, it would always be expected that this power would only be authorised by an appropriately trained and qualified individual.

13 In a situation where a patient is subject to a suspension certificate granted under sections 41(1), 53(1) or 127(1) of the Act, and where a condition has been attached to that suspension certificate to the effect that the patient is to be kept in the charge of an authorised person, then that authorised person can carry out certain actions separately from those described in paragraph 11 above. Those actions are:

- to take the patient into custody; and
- to resume the charge of the patient. If this is not appropriate or practicable, he/she may take the patient to any place considered appropriate by the patient's RMO.

14 Subsection (6) of section 303 allows the use of reasonable force where the actions described at subsections (1) and (2) of that section or paragraphs 10 and 13 above are being carried out. Reasonable force should only be used as a last resort where all other appropriate approaches not involving force have been exhausted. It will be important for practitioners to have regard to the principle set out at section 1(4) of the Act with respect to discharging functions under the Act in a manner which "involves the minimum restriction on the freedom of the patient that is necessary in the circumstances".

Inclusion of absconding provisions with Psychiatric Emergency Plans

15 It would be best practice for local agencies to include within their Psychiatric Emergency Plan ("PEP") contingency plans on the use of reasonable force with respect to absconding patients. The issues relating to absconding to be agreed upon in a PEP could include:

- the parties best placed within any specific locality to exercise reasonable force;
- the use of physical restraint, including handcuffs, batons or even firearms, depending on the level of threat offered by the patient (it would be expected that agreement would be reached on such matters taking into account guidelines published by relevant organisations such as the Mental Welfare Commission, the General Medical Council or the Royal College of Nursing, among others);
- the extent of the involvement of the police in any case of absconding; and
- suitable places where a patient may be taken into custody, where it is not immediately possible or appropriate to return the patient to hospital.

16 The timescales within which any of the actions described at section 303(1) and (2) and paragraphs 10 and 13 above can be carried out are laid out in subsection (4) of that section. These timescales are:

- if the patient is subject to a CTO, those actions can be carried out within 3 months of the day on which the patient absconded or within 3 months of the patient becoming liable to be taken into custody; and
- if the patient is subject to any other order, certificate or provision, those actions can be carried out at any point before the expiry of that order, certificate or provision.

chapter eight

How does a period of unauthorised absence affect the expiry date of a certificate, order or provision to which a patient is subject?

17 The patient's unauthorised absence does not affect the expiry date of any certificate, order or provision of the Act to which the patient was subject when the unauthorised absence began. However, there are some exceptions to this rule which are set out in sections 304(3) and 305 to 308 of the Act and in paragraphs 18 to 22 below.

18 Section 304(3) of the Act provides that if a patient's unauthorised absence lasts for more than 3 months, then the CTO to which he/she was subject ceases to have effect.

19 Section 305 of the Act provides for a scenario in which the period of unauthorised absence of a patient who is subject to a CTO lasts for more than 28 consecutive days but finishes at least 14 days before the expiry date of the CTO. In such circumstances, the CTO ceases to have effect 14 days after the patient's period of unauthorised absence ends. During this 14 day period after the period of unauthorised absence has ended, the patient's RMO must carry out a mandatory review of the CTO in terms of section 305(2) of the Act. Such a review must be carried out in accordance with the provisions of section 77(3) of the Act.

20 Section 306 of the Act provides for a scenario in which the period of unauthorised absence of a patient subject to a CTO finishes either on the day on which the CTO was due to expire or within 14 days prior to the day on which the CTO was due to expire. In such circumstances, the CTO continues for 14 days from the point at which the patient's period of unauthorised absence ended. During this 14 day period after the end of the period of unauthorised absence, the patient's RMO must carry out a mandatory review of the CTO in terms of section 306(2) of the Act. Such a review must be carried out in accordance with the provisions of section 77(3) of the Act.

21 Section 307 of the Act provides for a scenario in which the period of unauthorised absence of a patient subject to a CTO lasts for less than 3 months but finishes after the day on which the CTO was due to expire. In such circumstances, the CTO shall be treated as having continuing effect even after its expiry date and shall continue to have effect for a period of 14 days from the point where the patient's unauthorised

absence ended. During this 14 day period after the end of the period of unauthorised absence, the patient's RMO must carry out a mandatory review of the CTO in terms of section 306(2) of the Act. Such a review must be carried out in accordance with the provisions of section 77(3) of the Act. *(For further information on such a review see Chapter 7 of Volume 1 of the Code of Practice.)*

22 Section 308 of the Act provides for a scenario in which the period of unauthorised absence of a patient subject to a short-term detention certificate or a certificate granted under section 114(2) or 115(2) ends within 13 days of the date on which the certificate was due to expire. In such circumstances, the certificate continues to authorise the measures specified in it for a period of 14 days beginning with the day on which the patient's period of unauthorised absence ended.

chapter 9

transfers: patients within scotland (part 7, chapter 6)

chapter nine

Introduction

This chapter describes the processes attached to the transfer of certain categories of patients from one hospital to another.

Part 7 Chapter 6 of the Act deals with the transfer between hospitals in Scotland of a patient subject to a CTO. (Note that this chapter refers to transfers inside Scotland as "domestic transfers".) This chapter therefore outlines the basic procedures to be observed before moving on to a description of the process by which a patient or a patient's named person can appeal to the Tribunal against such a transfer.

The chapter concludes with an examination of how a patient who is subject to an emergency, short-term detention certificate or to an extension certificate may be transferred from one hospital to another within Scotland.

For information on the procedures to be followed where any patient is being transferred to or from Scotland under sections 289 or 290 of the Act, see Chapter 14 of Volume 1 of the Code of Practice.

Domestic transfer of a patient subject to a CTO (Part 7 Chapter 6)

01 The Act makes provision at section 124 for the domestic transfer of a patient subject to a CTO. In terms of section 124(3) of the Act, a domestic transfer may only take place where the managers of the receiving hospital have consented to the transfer taking place.

What practical considerations should be taken into account when transferring the patient?

02 The transfer should be carefully planned well in advance. The range of issues which should be considered by the members of the patient's multi-disciplinary team and by the managers of the sending and receiving hospitals include:

- ensuring that the patient, and his/her relatives, carers, named person, independent advocate and representatives have been informed of an agreed departure time in advance of the transfer, and ensuring that the patient is fully supported in preparing for the journey;
- providing an appropriate, swift and comfortable means of transport which is also suitable for the provision of medication, where necessary;

- anticipating any difficulties in relation to the required level of security and possible absconding en route (in as far as this is possible) bearing in mind the importance of caring for the patient in the manner which involves the minimum restriction on the patient's freedom that is necessary in the circumstances;
- ensuring that there is a clearly identified RMO in the receiving hospital;
- ensuring that the patient has a clearly identified MHO;
- ensuring that the receiving hospital has been informed of any relevant dates with respect to the Act's provisions, for example for consenting to medical treatment, or renewing a CTO;
- ensuring that staff in the receiving hospital are properly prepared for the patient's arrival and that time is taken to ensure that the patient can settle quickly into the new environment; and
- in the case of a patient aged under 18, that services are available in the receiving hospital which are appropriate to the needs of that patient.

Does any prior notice have to be given before the transfer takes place?

03 Yes.The managers of the hospital in which the patient is currently detained must in terms of section 124(4) of the Act give at least 7 days' notice of the proposed transfer to the following parties:
- the patient;
- the patient's named person; and
- the patient's primary carer.

04 Under sections 124(7) and 124(5) of the Act, hospital managers can waive this notification requirement where:
- the patient consents to the transfer, or
- if the patient has to be transferred urgently to another hospital (i.e. where there are strong clinical reasons for doing so).

05 In both these circumstances, the managers of the sending hospital must notify the patient, his/her named person and the patient's primary carer as soon as possible before the transfer takes place or, if this is not feasible, then as soon as possible after the transfer has taken place.In all cases, best practice is to ensure that as much advance notice is given as possible.

What happens if the transfer is delayed?

06 Nothing changes unless the proposed transfer does not take place within 3 months of the notice of the transfer being given to the patient; his/her named person; and his/her primary carer. If this 3 month period has elapsed, then the transfer can only proceed where additional conditions imposed by section 124(10) of the Act have been met. These additional conditions are:

- the managers of the receiving hospital continue to consent to the transfer of the patient; and
- the patient and his/her named person and primary carer have been given at least 7 days' notice of the transfer. (However, if the patient continues to consent to the transfer or if the transfer must take place urgently (that is, for strong clinical reasons), then this 7 days' notice requirement can be waived. Notification must also be given in those circumstances as soon as practicable before or after the transfer takes place.)

Who must be notified after the transfer has taken place?

07 The responsibility for notification rests with the managers of the transferring hospital. Under section 124(12) of the Act, the managers of the hospital from which the patient is transferred are required to notify the Commission of a range of matters within 7 days of the transfer taking place. These matters are:

- the date of the transfer;
- the name and address of the hospital to which the patient was transferred;
- whether 7 days' notice of the transfer had been given to the patient and his/her named person and primary carer; and
- if 7 days' notice was not given, why it was necessary to transfer the patient urgently and whether notice was subsequently given.

Can an appeal be made against a domestic transfer?

08 Yes. Sections 125 and 126 of the Act make provision for an appeal to be made to the Tribunal against a proposed domestic transfer. Section 125 provides for an appeal where the transfer is to a hospital other than a state hospital while section 126 provides for an appeal where the transfer is to a state hospital.

chapter nine

09 The right of appeal can be exercised by either the patient or the patient's named person where the patient has already received notice of the proposed transfer or where the transfer has already taken place. It is therefore important to note that an appeal can be made to the Tribunal even after a transfer has taken place.

10 It will be important for all members of the patient's multi-disciplinary team to make sure that the patient and the patient's named person are fully aware that they have a right to appeal against a domestic transfer. It would also be best practice for them to ensure that they provide the patient and the named person with information and assistance to enable them to exercise their rights, should they wish to do so.

What are the timescales within which an appeal must be made?

11 In the case of a patient, where he/she makes an appeal under section 125(3)(a) of the Act against a transfer to a hospital other than a state hospital, the timescales are as follows:

- if the patient received notice before the transfer took place, the appeal can be made at any point from the day on which notice was given up to 28 days after the transfer has taken place;
- if the patient received notice either on or after the day of the transfer, the appeal must be made within 28 days of the notice being given to the patient; and
- if the patient was not given notice of the transfer before it took place, the patient must make the appeal within 28 days of the transfer taking place.

12 In the case of the named person, if the appeal is made under section 125(3)(b) against a transfer to a hospital other than a state hospital, the timescales are as follows:

- if notice was given to the named person before the transfer took place, the appeal can be made at any point from the day on which notice was given to 28 days after the transfer; and
- if notice was given to the named person on or after the transfer, the appeal must be made within 28 days of the notice being given.

13 Where a patient or the patient's named person makes an appeal to the Tribunal under section 126(3) against a transfer to a state hospital, the same timescales apply as those described in the two preceding paragraphs except that the period of 28 days is replaced by the period of 12 weeks.

What are the possible outcomes of an appeal?

14 In terms of section 125(4) and section 126(4) of the Act, if an appeal is made against a domestic transfer, and if the transfer has not yet taken place, then the transfer may not go ahead unless the Tribunal gives its explicit approval for the patient to be transferred pending the appeal being determined.

15 In determining an appeal against a transfer to a hospital which is not a state hospital, the Tribunal can, in terms of sections 125(5), make an order:

- that the transfer should not take place; and
- where the transfer has already taken place, that the patient should be returned to the hospital from which the patient was transferred.

16 Where an appeal is made against a transfer to a state hospital, the Tribunal can in terms of section 126(5) make an order:

- that the transfer should not take place; and
- where the transfer has already taken place, that the patient should be returned to the hospital from which the patient was transferred.

17 The Tribunal can only make such an order where it is not satisfied that the following conditions are met:

- the patient requires to be detained in hospital under conditions of special security; and
- those conditions of special security can only be provided in a state hospital.

chapter nine

18 In the exceptional circumstances where a patient must be transferred to another hospital urgently for reasons of clinical necessity (for example, where the patient's condition has deteriorated rapidly) even though an appeal has been made to the Tribunal against the transfer, it would be permissible for the RMO in the sending hospital to grant a suspension certificate which would suspend the hospital detention requirement in the patient's CTO. Exceptional circumstances would indeed have to apply before such actions could be taken, and it would be best practice for the patient's RMO to always seek advice from the Mental Welfare Commission before granting the suspension certificate. *For further information on the process by which a suspension certificate can be granted in respect of a compulsory treatment order, see Chapter 4 of Volume 2 of the Code of Practice.*

Transferring patients subject to other certificates

19 A patient who is subject to an emergency detention certificate, a short-term detention certificate or an extension certificate can be transferred from one hospital to another. There are no formal procedures in the Act for the domestic transfer of such a patient. This is because a hospital is not specified in these certificates, in contrast to a CTO where a hospital must be specified in the order by way of section 66(1)(a). A patient subject to any of these detention certificates may therefore be transferred between two hospitals in Scotland without the need to comply with formal procedures under the Act.

20 Where it is proposed to transfer a patient to another hospital who is subject to such a detention certificate, it would be best practice to ensure, that:

- the transfer takes place, wherever possible, with the consent of the patient or the patient's named person;
- as much prior notice of the transfer as possible has been given to the patient, the patient's named person, the patient's MHO and other members of the multi-disciplinary team, and, subject to the patient's consent, their independent advocate and any carers and relatives of the patient; and
- due regard has been given to the same issues which are outlined in paragraph 2 above with respect to the transfer of a patient subject to a compulsory treatment order.

chapter 10
glossary of commonly used terms

chapter ten

Advance statement: this is a document drawn up in accordance with sections 275-6 of the Act. It is a written and witnessed document which is made when the patient is well and which sets out how s/he would prefer to be treated (or not treated) if s/he were to become ill in the future. The Tribunal and any medical practitioner treating the patient must have regard to the advance statement. A medical practitioner must also send to the Commission a written record of the reasons why the wishes set out in the advance statement have not been followed.

Assessment Order (section 52 of the 1995 Act): an order imposed by a criminal court prior to trial and/or after conviction before sentencing which authorises hospital detention for up to 28 days so that the patient's mental condition may be assessed. Medical treatment under Part 16 of the Act may be given to a patient in certain circumstances while subject to this order. It may be extended once only for a period of 7 days.

Approved medical practitioner: this is a medical practitioner who has been approved under section 22 of the Act by a Health Board or by the State Hospitals Board for Scotland as having special experience in the diagnosis and treatment of mental disorder. An approved medical practitioner will often be a consultant psychiatrist. Only an approved medical practitioner can grant a short-term detention certificate; and at least one of the two mental health reports forming part of a compulsory treatment order application must be provided by an approved medical practitioner.

Authorised person's warrant/a "section 292 warrant": this warrant authorises a person to enter the premises of another person where the person entering the premises has already been given the authority under another provision of this Act to take the person to another place or into custody. This could happen, for example, in a situation where a patient has absconded and a person who has been authorised under section 303 of the Act to take that patient into custody or to return them to hospital requires entry to the premises where the patient has been found.

Care plan: this is a document prepared by the patient's responsible medical officer under section 76 of the Act after a compulsory treatment order has been made. It lays out the forms of medical treatment and the other services the patient will be receiving while subject to the compulsory treatment order. This document should not be confused with the "proposed care plan" which is prepared under section 62 of the Act as part of the application for a compulsory treatment order.

chapter ten

Compulsion Order (section 57A of the 1995 Act): a final disposal imposed by a criminal court which authorises hospital detention or compulsory powers in the community for a period of 6 months, if not otherwise renewed. It may be renewed for six months and then annually thereafter. The procedures for the review of this order and for its renewal, variation and revocation are almost identical to those for a compulsory treatment order imposed under civil proceedings.

Compulsory treatment order: this is an order granted by the Tribunal under section 64(4) of the Act. It authorises any of the compulsory measures listed at section 66(1) for a period of six months, if not otherwise renewed. The compulsory treatment order can be renewed for six months, then for twelve months thereafter.

Designated medical practitioner: this is a medical practitioner appointed by the Mental Welfare Commission under section 233 of the Act. The function of a designated medical practitioner is to provide a second medical opinion with respect to certain medical treatments being given under Part 16 of the Act.

Emergency detention certificate: this is a certificate granted under section 36 of the Act. Where strict criteria have been met, it authorises the removal of a person to hospital within 72 hours and the detention of that person in hospital for a further 72 hours. An emergency detention certificate can be granted by any fully registered medical practitioner who has, where practicable, consulted and sought the consent of a mental health officer to the granting of the certificate.

Extension certificate: this is a certificate issued under section 47(1) of the Act. Where strict criteria have been met, it extends a period of short-term detention by three working days (not three calendar days) to allow for the preparation of an application for a compulsory treatment order.

Hospital Direction (section 59A of the 1995 Act): a final disposal imposed by a criminal court in addition to a sentence of imprisonment which allows the person to be detained in hospital initially for treatment for mental disorder and then transferred to prison to complete their sentence once detention is hospital is no longer required.

chapter ten

Independent Advocate: a person who enables the patient to express their views about the decisions being made about their care and treatment by being a voice for the patient and encouraging them to speak out for themselves. An independent advocate is employed by an advocacy organisation which is not directly funded or run by the Health Board or Local Authority. All people with mental disorder have a right to independent advocacy, not only those subject to compulsory measures.

Interim Compulsion Order: an order imposed by a criminal court after conviction and before sentencing which authorises hospital detention for assessment and treatment for a period of 12 weeks to allow further evidence to be obtained with respect to the person's mental disorder and the risk that they pose as a result of this disorder. It may be renewed regularly for up to one year.

Interim compulsory treatment order: this is an order granted by the Tribunal under section 65(2) of the Act. It authorises any of the compulsory measures listed at section 66(1) of the Act for a period of up to 28 days at a time. An unlimited number of interim orders can be granted as long as the total detention period authorised by the interim orders does not exceed 56 consecutive days.

Mental health officer's report: this is a report prepared under section 61 of the Act. It is prepared by the mental health officer as part of the application for a compulsory treatment order. It must detail background information on the person who is the subject of the application.

Mental health report: this is a report required under section 57(4) of the Act and prepared by a medical practitioner. Two such reports must form part of the application for a compulsory treatment order. The practitioner must lay out in this report the reasons why s/he believes that a compulsory treatment order is appropriate.

Multi-disciplinary team: this is the team providing care, treatment and support to the patient while they are in receipt of mental health services. The membership and nature of the team will necessarily vary according to the needs and circumstances of the patient. It would, however, be expected that the team would be made up of, where appropriate and relevant, medical practitioner(s), a mental health officer and other social workers, nursing staff/Community Psychiatric Nurses, psychologists, occupational therapists

chapter ten

etc. The team may also include community care service providers or voluntary organisations providing care and treatment. These components of the multi-disciplinary team would work together to co-ordinate and agree on all aspects of the patient's care and treatment. Multi-disciplinary working of a high quality will necessarily entail a genuine respect for the opinions of all members of the team; regular communication between all members of the team; and clearly defined information sharing processes.

Named person: this is someone nominated by a person in accordance with the provisions of Part 17 Chapter 1 of the Act to support them and protect their interests. The named person is entitled to receive certain information about the person and to act on behalf of the person in certain circumstances and at certain times set out in the Act.

Nearest relative: there are occasions in the Act where the nearest relative is given information about a person coming under the provisions of the Act, such as where a person is removed to a place of safety. Section 254 of the Act sets out a list of the people who will be considered in identifying a person's nearest relative.

Nurse's holding power: this is a power which can be exercised by nurses of a prescribed class by way of section 299 of the Act to hold a patient for up to 2 hours while awaiting a medical examination.

Place of safety: Section 300 defines a place of safety as a hospital, premises which are used to provide a care home services or any other suitable place (other than a police station) where the occupier is willing to temporarily receive a person with mental disorder. However, if no place of safety is available, a police officer may remove a person to a police station which should then be treated as a place of safety for the purposes of the person's detention.

Part 9 care plan: this is a document prepared by the patient's responsible medical officer under section 137 of the Act after a compulsion order has been imposed by a criminal court. It contains the same core information as the care plan of a patient who is subject to a CTO in that it sets out the forms of care and treatment for the mental disorder that the patient will receive while subject to the order but it also includes other information to take account of the status of the patient as a mentally disordered offender.

Proposed care plan: this is a document drawn up under section 62 of the Act by the mental health officer who is making the application for a compulsory treatment order. It contains details of the medical treatment for mental disorder, the community care services; and any other forms of care and treatment which it is proposed to provide to the patient if the compulsory treatment order is made. The "proposed care plan" should not be confused with the "care plan" which is prepared under section 76 of the Act by the patient's responsible medical officer subsequent to the making of a compulsory treatment order.

Removal order/"a section 293 warrant": an order granted by a sheriff or a justice of the peace under section 293(1) of the Act. It authorises certain persons to enter the premises of an individual at risk in order to remove them to a place of safety. It also authorises a constable to open lockfast places and the detention of the person for 7 days.

Restriction Order (section 59 of the 1995 Act): an order imposed by a criminal court in conjunction with a compulsion order with the effect that the measures specified in the compulsion order are without limit of time and the patient may not be granted leave or transferred to another hospital without the consent of the Scottish Ministers.

Section 35 warrants: these are warrants issued by a sheriff or a justice of the peace on an application from an MHO. The purposes for which these warrants can be granted are to enter premises; to detain a person in order to carry out a medical examination; and to allow a medical practitioner access to a person's medical records. There is no right of appeal against a warrant being granted or not being granted under section 35.

Section 68 detention period: this is a period of detention which lasts for five working days (not five calendar days). This detention period occurs automatically once an application for a compulsory treatment order has been submitted to the Tribunal. It begins on the expiry of a short-term detention certificate or an extension certificate, depending on which certificate the patient is subject to. The Tribunal must determine the compulsory treatment order application by the end of this section 68 detention period.

Section 86 determination: this is a determination made by the patient's responsible medical officer under section 86 of the Act to extend the compulsory treatment order without any variation of the compulsory measures or recorded matters specified in the order. A compulsory treatment order can be extended for six months, then for twelve months at a time thereafter. However, the Tribunal must review an order if it has not done so at any point within the previous two years. The Tribunal must also review section 86 determination if the mental health officer disagrees with this determination or if there is a difference between the type(s) of mental disorder stated in the section 86 determination and those in the compulsory treatment order.

Section 92 application: this is an application which the patient's RMO must make to the Tribunal under section 92 of the Act where s/he wishes to extend a compulsory treatment order with a variation of the compulsory measures or recorded matters specified in a compulsory treatment order.

Section 95 application: this is an application which the patient's RMO must make to the Tribunal under section 95 of the Act where s/he wishes to vary the compulsory measures or recorded matters specified in a compulsory treatment order.

Section 292 warrant: see "authorised person's warrant".

Section 293 warrant: see "removal order".

Short-term detention certificate: this is a certificate issued under section 44(1) of the Act. Subject to strict criteria, it authorises the conveyance of a person to hospital within 3 days of the certificate being granted, and then the detention in hospital of that person for a period of up to 28 days. A short-term detention certificate can only be granted by an approved medical practitioner with the consent of a mental health officer.

Social circumstances report: this is a report prepared by a mental health officer under section 231 of the Act. It must be produced within 21 days of any of the following events taking place: the granting of a short-term detention certificate; the making of an interim compulsory treatment order; a compulsory treatment order; an assessment order; a treatment order; an interim compulsion order; a compulsion order; a hospital direction; or a transfer for treatment direction. However, an MHO does not need to complete an SCR where s/he is satisfied that an SCR would serve little or no practical purpose. However, a record must be produced stating why the SCR is not being prepared. This record must be sent to the Mental Welfare Commission and to the patient's RMO.

Suspension certificate: this is a certificate granted under section 41, 53 127 or 128 of the Act. A suspension certificate granted under sections 41, 53 or 127 suspends the hospital detention requirement of an emergency detention certificate, a short-term detention certificate or a CTO respectively. A suspension certificate granted under section 128 can suspend any measure authorised in a CTO other than the hospital detention requirement. Under the Mental Health (Scotland) Act 1984, "suspension" was sometimes referred to as "leave of absence" or "being out on pass".

A suspension certificate may also be granted with respect to a patient who is subject to criminal justice proceedings. The processes involved in granting and revoking such a certificate are set out in Part 13 of the Act with the exception of a certificate with respect to a patient who is subject to a compulsion order without a restriction order; these are set out in section 127 as applied by section 179(1). Similar to CTOs, a suspension certificate granted under section 128 as applied by section 179(2) may suspend any measure in a compulsion order other than the hospital detention requirement.

Transfer for Treatment Direction: an order made by the Scottish Ministers under section 136 of the Act which allows the transfer of a prisoner to hospital for treatment of a mental disorder.

Treatment Order (section 52M of the 1995 Act): an order imposed by a criminal court which authorises hospital detention for treatment for mental disorder. Section 52R of the 1995 Act sets out the circumstances in which this order ceases to have effect.

chapter 11
forms

chapter eleven

All forms are non-statutory except where indicated

Form	Act reference	
		Short-term and Emergency detention (Parts 5 and 6)
DET 1	Sections 36 & 37	Emergency detention certificate
DET 2	Sections 44 & 45	Short term detention certificate
DET 3	Section 45	MHO duties under section 45
DET 4	Sections 47 & 48	Extension of short-term detention certificate
		Compulsory Treatment Order (Part 7)
CTO 1	Sections 63, 64 & 66	CTO application pack
CTO 1a	Sections 63, 64 & 66	CTO and Interim CTO admission form
CTO 2	Section 58	Mental health report
CTO 3a	Sections 77, 78 & 86	RMO's mandatory review of a CTO and section 86 determination to extend a CTO
CTO 3b	Sections 77, 78 & 86	Review by the Tribunal of a section 86 determination
CTO 4	Sections 78, 91, 92 & 103	RMO's mandatory review of a CTO and a section 92 application to extend and vary a CTO
CTO 5	Section 94	RMO's application to the Tribunal to vary a CTO
CTO 6	Section 65	The making of an interim CTO by the Tribunal
CTO 7	Section 112	RMO's record of a patient having been taken into custody following failure to attend for medical treatment where this is a compulsory measure in the CTO (this form may also be used for compulsion orders)
CTO 8	Sections 113, 117	RMO's record of the patient's non compliance generally with a CTO which authorises compulsory powers in the community (this form may also be used for compulsion orders)

chapter eleven

CTO 9	Sections 114 & 177	RMO's certificate authorising continued detention of the patient pending review or application for variation; or interim compulsory treatment order detention pending further review
CTO 10	Sections 96, 97	RMO's reference to the Tribunal with respect to the non-provision of a recorded matter and the Tribunal's determination with respect to such a reference
CTO 11	Section 98	Reference to the Tribunal by the MWC and the Tribunal's subsequent determination
CTO 12	Sections 105/106	Tribunal's determination where an interim extension and/or interim variation of the order is imposed
		Admission following criminal justice proceedings
ADM 1	Criminal Procedure (Scotland) Act 1995	Notification of admission of a patient following the imposition of an assessment order, a treatment order, an interim compulsion order, a supervision and treatment order, a compulsion order, a compulsion order and a restriction order, a hospital direction, a transfer for treatment direction or a probation order with a requirement for treatment for mental condition

		Discharge of a patient subject to criminal proceedings
DISC 1	Criminal Procedure (Scotland) Act 1995	Record of the discharge of a patient who is subject to: an assessment order, a treatment order, an interim compulsion order, a supervision and treatment order, a compulsion order, a compulsion order and a restriction order, a hospital direction, a transfer for treatment direction or a probation order with a requirement for treatment for mental condition.
		Review of an interim compulsion order (Part 8)
CO 5	53B(1) of CPSA 1995	RMO's report to the court where he/she considers that an interim compulsion order should be extended
		Compulsion Order (Part 9)
CO 1	Sections 149 and 167	RMO's application to the Tribunal to extend a CO following first review and the Tribunal's order following application
CO 2a	Sections 140, 152, 153 & 166	RMO's determination to extend a compulsion order following further review
CO 2b	Sections 140, 152, 153 & 166	Review by the Tribunal of the RMO's determination to extend a CO following further review
CO 3	Sections 157, 158 & 167	RMO's application to the Tribunal to extend and vary a CO and determination by the Tribunal following an application to extend and/or vary a CO
CO 4	Sections 160, 161 & 167	RMO's application to the Tribunal to vary a CO and the Tribunal's subsequent determination

chapter eleven

CO 6	Sections 168/169	Tribunal's determination where an interim extension and/or interim variation of a CO is imposed
CO 7	Sections 163, 164	Application by the patient or the named person to the Tribunal to revoke or vary a CO and the Tribunal's subsequent determination
CO 8	Sections 162/171	Reference to the Tribunal by MWC and the Tribunal's subsequent determination
CTO 7	Section 112 as applied by section 176	RMO's record of the patient having been taken into custody following failure to attend for medical treatment where this is a compulsory measure in the CO (or a CTO)
CTO 8	Sections 113 and 117 as applied by section 177	RMO's record of the patient's non compliance generally with a CO (or a CTO) which authorises compulsory powers in the community
CO 9	Section 114 as applied by section 177(2)	RMO's certificate authorising continued detention of the patient pending review or application for variation of a CO
CO 10	Sections 141, 142, 144	RMO's record of the revocation of a CO; a record of the notifications made with respect to the revocation and record of termination of a CO
		Compulsion Order and Restriction Order (Part 10)
CORO 1	Sections 183 & 185	RMO's review of a CORO
CORO 2	Sections 191, 193	Application by Scottish Ministers to Tribunal under section 191 or 193

CORO 3	Sections 193, 201 and 204	Tribunal's record of an application by the patient or named person against: – the variation by the Scottish Ministers of the conditions imposed by the Tribunal on the conditional discharge of the patient – being recalled to hospital by the Scottish Ministers and the Tribunal's subsequent determination of the application
		Hospital direction/Transfer for treatment direction (Part 11)
HD 1	Section 206	RMO's review of a hospital direction or a transfer for treatment direction
HD 2	Sections 210, 211, 213 to 215	The Scottish Ministers' record of their decision whether or not to revoke the direction following a recommendation by the RMO; their reference to the Tribunal where they have not revoked a direction after having received such a recommendation and their record of revoking the direction upon the instructions of the Tribunal. The Tribunal's record of the patient or named person having made an application under section 214 and of its own direction to the Scottish Ministers to revoke the direction
		Suspension of detention (Parts 5, 6, 7, 9 and 13)
SUS 1	Sections 127, 128 & 129	RMO's certificate granting the suspension of compulsory measures relating to a CTO, or an interim CTO

chapter eleven

SUS 2	Sections 41, 42, 53 & 54	RMO's certificate granting the suspension of an emergency detention certificate, or a short-term detention certificate and any subsequent revocation or suspension (where appropriate)
SUS 3	Sections 221 to 226	RMO's certificate granting the suspension of the measure authorising detention in hospital in accordance with sections 221 or 224 and revocation by the RMO or the Scottish Ministers of such a certificate.
SUS 4	Sections 127, 128, 129, as applied by 179	RMO's certificate granting the suspension of compulsory measures relating to a CO and the revocation of such a certificate
		Revocation of certificates (Parts 5, 6 and 7)
REV 1	Section 40	Revocation of emergency detention, short-term detention certificate and extension certificate
REV 2	Sections 72 & 80	RMO's revocation of a CTO or an interim CTO
REV 3	Section 119	RMO's revocation of a certificate granted under section 114 or 115 (applies to CTOs and COs)
REV 4	Sections 50, 100 & 120	Determination by the Tribunal following application by patient or named person to revoke a short-term detention certificate or a extension certificate ; or to revoke a section 114 or 115 certificate (as applicable to CTOs or COs); or to revoke or vary a CTO
		Transfers (Parts 7, 9, 12 and 18)
TX 1	Section 290	Cross-border transfer of a patient subject to civil or criminal justice proceedings

TX 2	Sections 124, 178 & 218	Notification by hospital managers of the transfer within Scotland of a patient subject to a CTO, a compulsion order, a compulsion order and a restriction order, a hospital direction or a transfer for treatment direction
TX 3	Sections 125, 126, 178, 219 & 220	Appeal by patient against transfer within Scotland
TX 4	Section 290	Tribunal determination following an appeal by the patient or named person against a cross-border transfer under section 290
		Social Circumstances Report (Part 15)
SCR 1	Section 231	Social circumstances report
		Medical treatment (Part 16)
T 1 (statutory)	Sections 235, 236 & 245	Safeguards for treatment by: certain surgical operations
T 2 (statutory)	Sections 238, 240 & 276	Certificate of consent to treatment
T 3 (statutory)	Sections 239, 241, 245 & 276	Certificate of second opinion for patients refusing consent of incapable of consenting, and record of section 276 requirements
T 4	Section 243	Urgent medical treatment
T 5	Section 248	Certificate safeguarding treatment to inform patients under 16
		Excessive security (Part 17)
EXS 1	Sections 264 & 265	Detention in conditions of excessive security
EXS 2	Sections 265, 266, 269 & 270	Order under sections 265, 266, 269 or 270 of the Act
EXS 3	Sections 267 & 271	Application to recall under sections 267 (264 – 266) and 271 (268 – 270) of an order made by the Tribunal
EXS 4	Section 291	Record of appeal under section 291 of the Act in relation to an unlawful detention

chapter eleven

		Nurse's holding power (Part 19)
NUR 1	Section 299	Nurse's power to detain pending medical examination
		Removal to a place of safety (Part 19)
POS 1	Section 298	Police constable's report: removal to a place of safety
		Warrants relating to the duty to enquire under section 33 (Part 4)
MHO 1 (statutory)	Section 35(1)	Application for warrant to enter premises
MHO 2 (statutory)	Section 35(4)	Application for warrant to enable medical examination
MHO 3 (statutory)	Section 35(7)	Application for warrant for medical practitioner to have access to medical records
		Warrants and Orders relating to entry detention and removal powers (Part 19)
MHO 4 (statutory)	Section 292 (Civil and Criminal)	Application by an authorised person to enter premises for the purpose of taking/retaking a patient
MHO 5 (statutory)	Section 293	Application to the sheriff for a removal order
MHO 6 (statutory)	Section 294	Application to a justice of the peace for a removal order
MHO 7 (statutory)	Section 295	Application for a recall or variation of a removal order

From September 2005, all Non Statutory forms and Statutory forms may be found on the Scottish Executive's website at www.scotland.gov.uk/health/mentalhealthlaw